KEYBOARD

MUSIC

KEYBOARD MUSIC

♦

Bernhard D. Weiser
University of Minnesota

WM. C. BROWN COMPANY PUBLISHERS
Dubuque, Iowa

Music Series

Consulting Editor

Frederick W. Westphal
Sacramento State College

Copyright © 1971 by
Wm. C. Brown Company Publishers

Library of Congress Catalog Card Number: 72—118646

ISBN 0—697—03407—0

Printed in the United States of America

To Eileen Bigelow, for her rare understanding of musicians

Preface

By virtue of its restricted size, this volume cannot be thorough. Countries are omitted which are musically significant. Canada, Japan, Australia, various Central and South American countries are neglected. Exigencies of space have dictated this seeming indifference. No lack of respect is intended.

Photographic illustrations of score fragments have not been included. It is our belief that they would not be practical for the nonmusician, while the reader who is seriously studying the art can find complete scores with ease.

Any art which has existed as long as the keyboard will have accumulated an enormous content. Even the large (and expensive) volumes can only refer to a minor portion of the music of almost four centuries. If this book kindles a desire in some readers to investigate the art in greater depth; if through its use they enlarge their collections of keyboard recordings and are tempted to attend keyboard concerts, it will have fulfilled the author's purpose.

People who write books are understandably enthusiastic about their life work and naturally wish to communicate this sentiment to others. The dismaying realization that they must cull from their many years of accumulated knowledge a coherent but minute collection of facts and from this construct a historical chain without broken links is daunting. If they agree to attempt the task it can only be attributed to a genuine desire, however foolhardy, to tell others of their own compulsive interest. Even though enthusiasm is frowned upon in academic writing, it must reveal itself despite the enthusiast's suppressive efforts. It is a feeling one cannot regret.

Thanks are due to Dr. Westphal for a substantial list of suggestions, every one valuable. Thanks are also due to Mrs. Helen Scherrer of the editorial staff of Wm. C. Brown Company Publishers for her gentle insistence on completion of this text. Authors who do not believe they should be authors must require such treatment and are only occasionally so favored.

Bernhard D. Weiser

Contents

KEYBOARD MUSIC

The Instruments

The capacities of man have still to be fully measured. Among his many capabilities is that one called musical expression, representing a need to communicate something for which words cannot suffice. To express this type of communication, primitive man sang.

At one time he blew through a hollow reed and founded the woodwind family of instruments. He forced air from tightly compressed lips, through the small end of a hollowed animal's horn, and thereby founded a family of instruments later called the brass family (because of the replacement of the horn by metal). He plucked at a tautened gut string and later drew a taut thread across the stretched string and founded two families of stringed instruments, one using the fingertips or a small plectrum with a twanging result, the other using a bow for a prolonged singing sound. Finally, he made sound by percussion or striking his fingers, palm, or fist against a hollowed log or piece of hide stretched around a hollowed gourd. He substituted a mallet for his hand and thereby began to make music for the first time by a kind of lever which was an extension of his own arm. Then it occurred to him to use the hammer on the taut gut string to make a veritable tone, not a very low and indistinct approximation of the earlier drum sound.

From these primitive beginnings to the highly complicated system of levers in the modern piano, the history of keyboard music and the instruments on which it is played is a little like the history of science, with most of the progress being made in only the last several hundred years of man's history. In this comparatively short time, man has made his instruments and the music for them prodigiously varied and highly complicated. This book will tell the history of one branch of the family of percussion instruments, the branch which resulted in the piano.

We have all seen a keyboard, with its symmetrical grouping of white and black notes. When any key is depressed, a pitch is heard, but we rarely examine the mechanism by which the sound is created. We rarely ask ourselves why the sound persists, though in diminishing volume, as long as the key remains depressed, nor why the sound vanishes the instant our finger releases the key, nor why a pedal depressed by our foot will cause the sound to persist even if our finger releases the key. We have ten fingers and can make ten simultaneous sounds by depressing ten keys at once, which is quite a good argument for developing such an instrument, since no instrument played by one performer can sound so many pitches at once, except one other, the organ.

THE PSALTERY, THE DULCIMER

The remotest ancester of the keyboard instrument had no keyboard but it did have the strings that were later attached to the keyboard. It was called a psaltery (silent "p"). The strings were plucked with the fingers, and it probably antedated a large family of eastern European zithers, west European lutes, harps, lyres, certainly the comparatively modern guitar, and the keyboard family. What followed it most closely and yet represented a development or evolution of the psaltery was the dulcimer, not radically different but played in another fashion. This time the strings, instead of being plucked by the fingertips, were struck by one or two padded hammers wielded by the performer.

This whole family of instruments may be described as a group of strings, usually gut, stretched tightly above a sound-magnifying hollow drum. Part way along each string it might be made more taut by wedging a small upright piece of wood or metal between the string and the drum or sound box surface. This is called a bridge, and it serves to elevate the string appreciably above the drum surface. The strings can be tightened or loosened by winding each about a peg. The tighter it is wound, the higher the pitch will sound when the string is plucked (psaltery style) or struck (dulcimer style). This peg is still in existence for every type of instrument having strings, whether they are gut as in the violin or wire as in the piano. When a performer wished to play pitches other than those represented by the untouched strings, he was at liberty to press his finger at one end of a string, thereby changing its length and tension and thence its pitch. If he used one hand for this purpose, he could use his remaining hand only to pluck or strike, thus limiting the sounds he could make to

Figure 1. Seventeenth-Century Dulcimer, played with hand-held hammers, the H. Boddington Collection, London. (From Dr. A. Buchner's **Musical Instruments Through the Ages,** p. 212.)

what one hand alone might pluck or strike. This limitation led very clearly to the conception of the keyboard, where both hands could be free to make sounds, and, as in the case of the organ, both feet could be added for the same general purpose of expanding the means of playing.

THE CLAVICHORD

It was not until somewhere around the twelfth century that the first keyboard instrument was generally known. By this time a comparatively large number of strings would be stretched across a sound-magnifying or resonating wooden case, and the lever or key by which the sound could be produced was connected at one end to an upright piece of wood or metal. Just as in a teeter-totter, the finger pressed the key, at the other end the upright, called a tangent, rose and impacted against and clung to the string. A very small, delicate pitch could be heard, diminishing into a tiny residue of sound. The instrument was called a clavichord—the first part of the word meaning key, the second part representing a harmonious group of simultaneous sounds.

The clavichord shape was oblong. The strings ran in parallel lines from left to right as the performer sat at the keyboard. It had no legs to stand on and could be set down on a tabletop. Its lightness, its small size, and its very small volume of sound had an advantage, in that it could be played at one end of a room without disturbing unduly the people at the other end.

The clavichord brought not only delight but quite a few headaches in the form of mechanical problems to be solved. One was the fact that there was not room for a separate string for every note. An ingenious solution was contrived whereby one string could be made to serve two or more keys of the keyboard, though that meant that certain notes could not be simultaneously sounded. Another problem had to do with accuracy of pitch. Before this, the pitch was determined by the pressing of a fingertip at a certain spot near one end of the taut string, and if the spot was not exactly chosen, it could be easily changed to make a slightly higher pitch or one slightly lower. In the clavichord, however, the pitch of each string was fixed in advance and could not be changed without ceasing to play, while the performer laboriously "tuned" each string by tightening or loosening a peg around which was wound one end of the string. A scientific controversy arose concerning the fixed pitch of each note, one which was not settled until fairly late in the eighteenth century, some six hundred years later. Music peculiarly suited to the instrument was also slow to arrive. For a long time, the clavichord had no individuality and was either played along with other instruments in what is called ensemble, or else played music that was written for several voices in what is called a transcription. It was not until the seventeenth century that music was composed exclusively for it.

The clavichord was—and is—a percussion instrument, and the kind of sound caused by a blow against a string was not necessarily the most popular sound. Actually, after singing, the most popular sound was—and still is all over the world—the plucked string sound. So it is not surprising that a keyboard was adapted to do what so many people wanted; namely, to be able to make many simultaneous plucked string sounds, and also to be able ultimately to play with greater rapidity than could be achieved by the fingertip plucking each separate note, and still later, to be able to extend the range (i.e., play higher and lower) beyond that permitted on the usual plucked string instrument.

THE LUTE

In western Europe, the great favorite in plucked string instruments was the lute. From the time of the earliest medieval troubadour or wandering composer-performer, the picture is only complete if we envision him with his beautiful long-necked gourd-bodied lute with as few as four or as many as ten or more strings. The lute was so popular that almost everyone of gentle birth learned to play it, and with so very many performers, a most complicated technical ability developed and performers' fame spread over wide areas.

Ornamentation

The lute looked beautiful; the appearance of the performer while playing it was graceful, and it sufficed for the accompaniment of solo or single person singing. When it was played by itself as a solo instrument, however, it revealed a short-lasting sound for each plucked note, not very resonant, a sound musicians term as "dry." Because of this, many unplayed strings were added to vibrate in sympathy with the played strings and add depth of sound, volume, and resonance. They did not completely solve the duration-of-sound problem sufficiently to please the performers, so the performers, most of whom were composers who played their own as well as other composers' works, began to write or improvise intermediate notes to fill the gap left by the cessation of the short-lived sound. They tremoloed, which consists of vibrating the fingertip or plectrum against the string on one pitch for a note they desired to be long lasting. They wrote trills, consisting of two rapidly alternating notes for the same purpose. They filled the gaps by playing a profusion of notes extraneous to the melody; these came to be known as ornaments and were later codified and recorded in "tables" with a set symbol for each ornament and an appropriate name for each. Besides this, they played their chords not as simultaneous plucking of several strings, but as separated individually plucked notes played from lowest to highest or vice versa, and gave it the term "style brisé" or broken-voiced style.

These interpolated notes grew steadily in variety and number during the history of the lute and its keyboard successor, the harpsichord. At first improvised, then codified and set down by composers in "tables" or schematics like a blueprint, they were indicated by short-hand symbols, illustrated and explained. They became important enough to be considered indispensable and assumed regional characteristics so that the Italian type of ornamentation was distinct from the French. At certain periods, the ornamentation became so profuse that it tended to "swamp" the melodies, resulting in artificiality. It obscured the clear rhythmic outline, and what had begun as a simple forthright tune instead became, with ornamentation, a complex tangle of clustered notes and rhythms hardly to be grasped by any but the most sophisticated musicians.

At this distance in time, we can appreciate the beauties of ornamentation in the different types of early music. The English composers never made tables of their ornaments and we are at a loss to be specific in the performance of Elizabethan ornamentation. The Italian style had no ornament symbols but from what we read and see illustrated in the old treatises, we understand that the Italian ornamentation actually resulted in the metamorphosis of a melody into what we now call a "variation"; that is, a sufficient alteration through inserted scales, arpeggios, and broken chords in rhythmic patterns sufficient to justify the term.

THE HARPSICHORD

To play all of the above cited ornaments on the lute called for prodigious ability. It seems logical, therefore, that when a keyboard instrument was devised with a plucked string quality, it gradually superseded the lute, since it could make all the lute sounds, play all the lute ornaments, easily allow two or more melodies to be simultaneously performed, had a longer lasting and larger volume of sound, and only suffered the disadvantage of not being able to be slung about the neck by a pretty ribbon. This instrument was the harpsichord. By the middle of the fifteenth century it had reached a point in its development where it might be said to be universally accepted as here to stay. It was not until two hundred more years had passed, however, that it can be considered to have edged out the lute which declined rapidly in the seventeenth century.

The harpsichord became a beautiful piece of furniture with a characteristic "wing" shape, and it is from this harpsichord shape that our well-known grand piano is designed. The strings were also placed similar to our grand piano, running straight ahead of the performer at the keyboard, though not crossing above or below each other as do the lower and longer piano strings. The cabinet which housed the mechanism was beautifully made by the finest cabinet makers of the sixteenth through the eighteenth centuries, and for wealthy aristocratic people, the services of fine painters were enlisted to decorate the cabinets with scenes and patterns.

But the interior to a musician must have been far more fascinating. For every key of the keyboard, there was more than one string, since by manipulating either a foot or a hand lever, the same key could

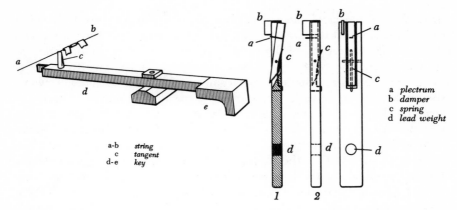

Figure 2. Left—The striking mechanism of the clavichord; Right—The striking mechanism (jack) of the harpsichord (from Geiringer's **Ancient Instruments**)

play any one of three pitches set an octave apart from each other. This meant that three separate strings were needed and these were placed in three layers, with the shortest string (for the highest note) in the lowest layer. Some harpsichords had only two strings thus arranged, some had as many as four. For each string a sound-producing device was needed; this was called a jack and so each key controlled at least two and sometimes as many as four jacks. The harpsichord suffered one great deficiency. It could make little or no gradation of sound from soft to loud. Whether you gently pressed a key on the keyboard or pounded it, there would be so little difference in the volume of sound produced as to render it monotonously uniform. However, by various methods and mechanisms, this deficiency was disguised. The harpsichord usually had two keyboards instead of one as in a piano. Of course, smaller-sized harpsichords frequently had to make do with only one keyboard or "manual," as it is termed in harpsichord and organ nomenclature. In the full-sized harpsichord, it was possible, by a foot or hand lever, to couple the two manuals so that playing on one would cause the identical note on the other to play, thus doubling the volume. Another lever could add the "4-foot" or octave higher string to be sounded and still another could cause the "16-foot" or octave lower string to be added, thus creating a volume four times as great as the originally sounded single note through the addition of three more sounds.

The jacks which created these sounds were very ingenious devices. When a key was pressed, an upright pole at the opposite end rose and closely passed vertically next to the desired string. Sticking out from this pole was a "plectrum" or small piece of quill or leather. As the pole rose next to the string, this plectrum caught the string and twanged it in passing. Having passed, and the key being released by the finger, the pole (or jack) descended past the string. A clever hinge caused the sticking-out plectrum to fold up so it did not twang the string on the way down. Another piece of mechanism caused the string to be muffled once the key was let go so that it would not go on vibrating (and sounding) and cause a discordant mixture of sound with other vibrating strings.

The wonder is that the performer could learn to cope with all the intricacies of both these basic keyboard instruments. The problems in instruments have never ceased. In the clavichord-harpsichord days, strings made of the prevalently poor metal snapped easily, mainly through changes in humidity and temperature rather than through playing. Sound boards (that part of the box especially calculated to vibrate sympathetically for enlarging and prolonging the string vibration) warped and cracked; the wooden frame of the instrument, having to bear the torsion of all these tightly stretched strings, warped also. The strings, as a result of all these wood twistings, loosened or tightened beyond the calculated tightness for a particular pitch and consequently had to be frequently retuned. Performers became their own tuners and repair men.

THE SPINET, THE VIRGINALS

The harpsichord took on various shapes, dictated by costs, social habits, limitations of space, and specific desires on the part of the performers. A kind of small harpsichord, called a spinet, was one offshoot of the parent instrument. This was shaped like a triangle and was at times five-sided through the chopping off of two of the corners, with the strings running diagonally. There was only one string reserved for each note, the keyboard usually had fewer notes (about fifty) than the large harpsichord, but still the plucking mechanism was the same. In England, during the last half of the sixteenth and first third of the seventeenth centuries, the virginals was the favorite harpsichord-type keyboard instrument. Like the spinet, it contained only one string for each note. The earliest models were actually small enough to rest comfortably on the performer's lap; as they grew more important, larger models were placed on tables, and finally they stood on their own three or four legs. The virginal shape was oblong, precisely like that of the clavichord, though like all the harpsichord types it still played through the medium of plucked strings. The prevalent use of this instrument by the Elizabethan composers (those living during and sometime after Queen Elizabeth's reign) gave an enormous impetus to idiomatic keyboard music. By "idiomatic" keyboard music, we mean music that could be played to sound well only on the keyboard and would be awkward to play when essayed on another instrument.

The Harpsichord Makers

We should list the names of some famous harpsichord makers, though they will remain only names to us, since we cannot hear their products. Perhaps the most famous "house" or factory was Ruckers of Antwerp, who, for several generations, led the field in harpsichord manufacture. In France, Taskin was perhaps the best known; in Italy, Spinetti, from whose name many believe (and we think wrongly) the name of spinet is derived. Cristofori, who is to be discussed in relation to the first pianoforte, was primarily a harpsichord maker. In Germany, the Silbermann family, like the Ruckers in Belgium, achieved fame through its association with the Bach family. Many more might be mentioned but their names are not sufficiently significant to our history.

We feel that we know more about the piano because it is still the prevalently used keyboard instrument. Its start is as recent as the beginning of the eighteenth century. It would be well here to state that a change of instrument such as that of the harpsichord-clavichord types to the piano does not automatically imply a change for the better. There were good reasons for the change; neither the clavichord nor the harpsichord could fulfill all the aspirations of the composers, but then neither could the piano. Let us say that the clavichord and harpsichord fulfilled certain aspirations and that the piano was needed to fulfill others. We will discover these differences as we proceed.

THE PIANOFORTE

About the year 1709 Bartolomeo Cristofori, an Italian, built a pianoforte or fortepiano. Forte means loud, piano soft, so the term already gives a clue to the builder's aspiration—to make a keyboard instrument that would play both volumes. Actually, the harpsichord could be played loud and soft, but had never succeeded in permitting the performer to play gradations of sound, swelling from soft to loud and vice versa. It was almost the only instrument with this limitation, so it is no wonder that performers and composers professed themselves not completely satisfied with it. They "pressured" the instrument makers to solve the problem and, as we know, the pianoforte was born. The clavichord was indeed able to make volume gradation, but since this volume gradation could be thought of as the equivalent of a whisper (from a very soft to a loud whisper, but still a whisper), it could not serve the desired purpose. What was desirable was a mechanism that would make it possible to strike a key with greater or lesser force and achieve an equivalently greater or lesser volume of sound. On the clavichord, there was a further disadvantage. The tangent that struck the string (once the finger struck the key) really only "pushed" the string and then stuck to it, resulting in the aforesaid "whisper" of sound, and that sound's duration, because of its initial "whisper," was momentary. What was needed was a blow on the string by a suitably padded object (to avoid harshness); then the padded object had to fall away immediately from the vibrating string which volume of sound would gradually diminish unless "dampened" or muffled by a piece of felt dropping onto the string upon the removal of the finger from the key. If this sounds complicated, then remember that this is exactly what happens when the piano is played, and therefore the mechanism for fulfilling it required much ingenuity.

Cristofori's inventiveness showed in that part of the mechanism called the escapement. When the key is finger-struck, the padded hammer at the other end bounds upward, strikes the string, and falls back to its original position, though the finger is still holding the key down. The performer finds it desirable to hold the key down, since in doing so, the "damper" or sound-muffling piece of felt is kept suspended above the string, allowing it to continue to vibrate until, on releasing the key, the damper drops onto the string, cutting short its residue of

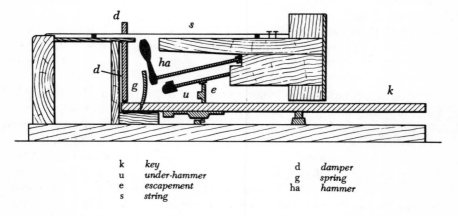

k	key	d	damper
u	under-hammer	g	spring
e	escapement	ha	hammer
s	string		

Figure 3. Cristofori's piano striking mechanism (the action) (from Geiringer's **Ancient Instruments**)

sound. Besides the above, the volume of sound can be graded, the harder the finger-blow, the louder the sound.

The announcement of this invention did not electrify the keyboard playing world. This early piano had distinct differences and drawbacks. To many, the sound, different than any they were accustomed to, was unpleasant. Not until the days of Mozart and Beethoven did the real encouragement come from the most important musical sources. Broadwood, England's greatest piano builder, travelled to Vienna to consult with Beethoven for ideas on the development and improvement of his piano, and Stein of Vienna did the same with Mozart. But this was between seventy-five and one hundred years after the invention first appeared.

Since Cristofori was a harpsichord maker, he used the familiar wing shape for the new piano. As we have noted, this is similar to the shape of the grand piano today. It was not too long after the piano's acceptance that another shape, based on the clavichord idea, was developed, the so-called "square" piano, which in reality was oblong and had the strings running from left to right as in the clavichord and virginal. The only advantage of the square piano was the saving of room space, an important factor when the piano was to be placed in the (usually) small room of a private home. Eventually, even the square piano was made still smaller by creating the upright piano, again for the purpose of saving more space. In this, the strings ran vertically from above the performer's head almost to the floor. The upright piano has never been seriously regarded as an instrument for public solo performance, but only for practice and as a home or parlor convenience.

Pianoforte Music

With all the resistance to the acceptance of the new pianoforte, one might well ask how the piano survived at all. Let us see what it had in its favor. Foremost in this list might be the desire of the music-loving and therefore the music-making public's desire for different kinds of music than any heretofore in vogue. In the emerging non-polyphonic (without several simultaneous melodies) music, the new pianoforte's thicker tone, greater resonance, and louder volume proved an advantage. Music of "feeling," variously called "sentiment," "empfindsamkeit," "gallant style," demanded these pianistic rather than harpsichordistic or clavichordistic qualities. Music that could be thick with feeling, strongly dramatic, bombastic, and finally virtuosic or possessing a show-off quality, ran high in the public's favor in the nineteenth century.

Improvements in the Pianoforte,
Eighteenth and Nineteenth Centuries

Once the pianoforte, or as it is now known, the piano, gained some ascendancy, the composers began to write exciting idiomatic compositions for it. From the sentimental, elegant style, they went on to ever more dramatic, fiery, and faster music in one direction and more slow melting music in the opposite direction. Inevitably, the piano was improved. Its range (the length of its keyboard) climbed from 5 to 6½, then 7 octaves, and finally to its present 7 octave plus 3 note range. You have read of the ingenious escapement invented by Cristofori. Now a double escapement was created by a Frenchman, Erard, in the 1820's. This device, like the single escapement, not only made the hammer drop away from the string with the finger still depressing the key, but it made the hammer drop only a small distance instead of all the way back to its rest position. Then, if the key was struck repeatedly and rapidly, the hammer could respond each time, making fast repeated notes and trills possible. Foot pedals for keeping the dampers raised for tone sustaining had already been invented and now a "soft" pedal, called una corda (single string) pedal, was added. Since the hammer now struck as many as three unison-tuned strings at a time for greater tone amplitude or volume, this "soft" pedal moved the whole keyboard minutely to the right, permitting the hammer to strike either two or even one string only, thus making the volume as small as one-half or one-third as much as before the pedal was pressed. Much later (at the end of the nineteenth century), a third "middle" pedal was added. Called the sostenuto pedal, it contrived to hold aloft one damper only at will, so that one note might be sustained throughout a passage. Cross-stringing was another "first" developed in the piano. Since the length of a string, its thickness and degree of tautness or tension, all have a bearing on its volume, quality

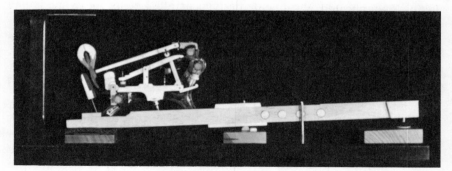

Figure 4. Modern piano action (courtesy of Steinway and Sons Company).

of sound and pitch, it stands to reason that of two strings, the one which has more metal by reason of its length will have a richer sound. But it is very impractical to keep extending the overall length of the piano to achieve this richness. So instead, someone hit upon the idea of having the strings crisscross in the lower register, thus enabling more strings to be long.

Perhaps the greatest single invention concerning the piano after the double escapement was the arrival, finally, of the heavy metal framework to hold all of these tightly-drawn metal strings. If all the strains on all the strings of the modern piano are added together, a total stress of tons of tension results, and all of this must be contained within the circumference of the metal frame. Without it, strings would have to be thinner, fewer, shorter, and slacker, which is precisely the case in the older harpsichord and clavichord. Now, thanks to the metal frame, more stress can be applied to heavier strings to pull them up to desired pitches. Few refinements have followed, though these few are important. At one time, during the first half of the nineteenth century, strings broke all too easily and so frequently in concert performances that often a person would be stationed at the side of the instrument to haul the broken strings out of the way of those still whole. Now, thanks to improved metals and alloys, this very rarely happens. Now, too, fine copper wire is wound very tightly and closely around the bass (or lower) strings, because it has been found that this results in a lower pitch and more beautiful sound than the brass formerly used.

Pitch and Temperament

Every stringed instrument presents a continuing problem in pitch control since the natural variations of humidity and temperature make impossible a constantly exact tension of the string. The problem is further complicated in the case of the keyed instrument by the difficulty in finding the exact pitch for each string. This must be dwelt upon as it is peculiar to the keyboard.

We are all familiar with and take for granted correct pitch. When we hear a "sour" note on a bowed instrument or in a vocal performance, we dismiss it wryly with the hope and expectation that it will not recur. Since the pitch of a keyboard note is preset, however, we know it must recur if it happens at all. The earliest keyboard intervals were limited to about seven in number, best represented by the white keys on the keyboard before they begin to repeat the design of "do" to "do" an octave higher. As music became more sophisticated, difficulties multiplied. There were simply an insufficient number of pitches, and so two were added, a half step above the fourth step of the scale, or "F♯," and a half step below the seventh step, or "b♭." The real complications began to throng when chords, or the simultaneous sounding of several pitches, were attempted, when more pitches were introduced to the number of twelve where it rests at present, and when the music essayed to go higher in register by several octaves than the original octave, and equally lower. The complication was caused by the dismaying realization that "sour" sounds were resulting from many of the pitch combinations. It is a tribute to the ingenuity of the theorists and musicians from the middle ages to the beginning of the eighteenth century that they were aware of the problem and ceaselessly sought a solution.

Elaborate calculations were made and discoveries resulted concerning pitch relationships. A vibrating string was known to vibrate in its parts as well as a whole, the smaller the vibrating part resulting in higher and fainter sound. These sounds were plotted and charts made of a great gamut of primary and partial pitches.

Three chronological solutions were applied. The first, since called the "just" system, worked quite well with the earliest, abbreviated scale of seven to nine tones. When the scale was expanded and more sophisticated tone combinations were tried, the "mean tone" system was adopted. This worked well to only a limited degree since many scales and certain chords had to be sedulously avoided because of the "sour" sounds which ensued with their use. Finally, with a resignation born of the realization that an ideal solution is impossible, a system of almost complete compromise was adopted, one in which all the notes of a scale, with the exception of the octave, are deliberately mistuned, but the calculated distortion is so slight for each note that the human ear is almost completely unaware of the violations. The compromise system is called "well-tempered."

Touch and Technique

We have five fingers on each hand and today we find it difficult to understand why the early performers did not find it desirable to use all five fingers. Yet it is true that as late as the eighteenth century, the right hand thumb and little finger were rarely used, rapid consecutive notes going up and down the keyboard were often played by using only two adjacent inner fingers. Only when a chord or a large stretch from low to high note occurred were the end fingers called into play. As an innovation, the hand finally was cupped on the keyboard in the same shape that it normally assumes when hanging at one's side and as it is now universally positioned. This shape was used exclusively in playing the clavichord and subsequently the piano. The harpsichord hand position, even today as in its heyday, favors flattened knuckles as an aid to equality of finger pressure. This is desirable in the performance at an instrument which would derive no advantage from finger inequality since its volume of sound is uniform regardless of pressure. The clavichord, on the other hand, was so susceptible of nuance, both in volume and quality, that the individual finger thickness and length could be exploited in performance and developed in practice. The harpsichord, with its louder and more metallic sound, evoked a brilliant concept in speed, rhythmic drive, and passage work of many closely-spaced notes. The clavichord lent itself to slower, lyric, tender, legato (or connected) melodic and harmonic constructions, and the techniques for the two instruments were, therefore, adapted to these varied ends.

When the pianoforte began to emerge as an instrument which was to supersede the others, it began to alter and remold the technical approach to the keyboard. Because it could play louder and softer

Figure 5. Clavichord, decorated in Chinese (red) style. In 1888, it belonged to Mr. Gerald Wellesley of London. (From Hipkins **Musical Instruments,** plate 32.)

than the clavichord in direct ratio to the pressure applied to each key, more than the natural weight of the finger was required. The weight of the arm was called into play. The technique which had to be developed to allow for and control this weight application at varying speeds required a concept transcending the fingers alone and including the arm and the torso. Exercises or études (studies) for developing strength and speed were composed; the finger equalization of the harpsichord technique was combined with the cupped or arched hand of the clavichord technique. The modern piano is a large and heavy instrument whose sound is expected to fill halls containing from a few hundred to thousands of seats. The muscular apparatus of the modern performer is adapted to this end. He has developed great strength in the individual finger muscles and has learned the science of arm weight and even back weight application to notes and chords. He has had to pay a price for this, as has also his audience. The harpsichord and more particularly the clavichord were never performed for large gatherings. It was not the custom, nor could their sound be heard clearly in large premises. The intimacy created by the minute sound developed in performer and listener a degree of aural refinement which has been lost since its replacement by the piano.

TITLES

Titles in art can be misleading. They tend, as do all printed words, to foreshadow in our minds the art product before we have experienced it. Some are of the opinion that titles limit the imagination which, without the title as a guide, would act freely to conjure up for each listener a completely subjective reaction. We must recognize, however, that titles can have a function which is technical and descriptive of the form or the style. Thus, in painting, the term Impressionist describes a style which quickly came to be recognized in the application of a brush technique depicting melting outlines, subtle nuances of color, and a deliberate obscurity of form. Titles in music range from the bare labeling of a form without regard to emotional content to a style evoking the expectation of the tempo and lilt of a particular dance; from a character piece describing a single person to a popular tune title.

All of the above types of title appeared in the earliest keyboard examples. They were meant for purposes of clarification but there were times when they caused confusion. The confusion arose because titles, like so many other things, underwent change as a result of the passage of time and geographical location. The title "fugue" meant "canon" or "round" originally, as in Three Blind Mice; later it became the title of a highly complex and beautifully shaped piece of the late Baroque period. The word "sonata" meant a piece which was "sounded" or played on an instrument, in contrast to a "cantata" which was any sung piece. The sonata went through many changes, however, from a single short piece in two halves to a grouping of several short pieces to a monumental construction of three to five linked movements.

In successive chapters, titles will be dealt with at length, and it will be well to remember that any title which is discussed has a meaning most particularly for its time and place, so that a special effort must be made by the reader to clarify this detail. It is so easy to fall into the error of assuming that the Fantasy of the middle Baroque period is the equivalent in shape and emotional significance of a Fantasy by Chopin. Nothing could be worse than this assumption, since the middle Baroque fantasy is a strictly constructed piece of contrapuntal (or imitative) texture, while Chopin's is a free, almost improvised, and loosely-structured piece which has the emotional scope of an untrammeled dream.

SUGGESTED READING

Bach, C. P. E. *Essay on the True Art of Playing Keyboard Instruments.* Translated by W. Mitchell. New York: W. W. Norton & Company, Inc., 1949, pp. 41-46 (fingering); pp. 30-40 (general observations on technique and taste, tuning, etc.).

Closson, E. *The History of the Piano.* Translated by D. Ames. London: Paul Elek, 1947, pp. 13-21 (clavichord); pp. 35-42 (harpsichord); pp. 54-60 (tuning and pitch); pp. 77-81 (grand piano); pp. 88-90 (square piano).

Dolmetsch, A. *The Interpretation of the Music of the 17th and 18th Centuries.* London: Novello and Co., Ltd., 1946, pp. 88-92 (ornamentation); pp. 488-493 (ornament symbols).

Grout, D. J. *A History of Western Music.* New York: W. W. Norton & Company, Inc., 1960, p. 202 (the lute).

Harich-Schneider, E. *The Harpsichord.* Kassel: Barenreiter, 1954.

Neupert, H. *Harpsichord Manual.* Kassel: Barenreiter, 1960, pp. 9-25 (general discussion of harpsichord family).

Neupert, H. *The Clavichord.* Kassel: Barenreiter, 1965, pp. 38-61 (the clavichord as a musical instrument).

SUGGESTED WRITTEN ASSIGNMENTS

1. As predecessors of keyed instruments, state the difference between the dulcimer and the psaltery.
2. Name at least three characteristics of construction and sound which differentiate the clavichord from the harpsichord.
3. Name two reasons for the decline of the lute in popularity.
4. What is meant by free-voiced style?

5. Name two advantages possessed by the harpsichord over the piano and/or the clavichord.
6. Why was the pianoforte slow in achieving popularity?
7. Name five improvements in piano construction from the time of its appearance until the present.
8. What problems faced the early performer in the control of pitch?
9. Name the three types of tuning and explain their differences.
10. What is the advantage of using the finally evolved system of tuning?
11. Name the differences in finger usage and hand position as applied to the clavichord, harpsichord, and the piano.
12. How does piano technique differ from its predecessors in muscular usage and development?
13. What was the purpose of introducing ornaments in lute performance?
14. What is the difference between division (or Italian) ornamentation and the French type?
15. Explain the paradox of titles both clarifying and confusing the music performer.

SUGGESTED LISTENING

1. BACH, J. S.—The Two-Part Inventions (recorded on the clavichord, the harpsichord, and the piano).
2. FROBERGER—*Lamentation for Ferdinand IV* (clavichord).
3. FRESCOBALDI—*Toccata d'Intavolatura* (harpsichord).
4. CHOPIN—Etudes, Opus 10, No. 4 and No. 5 (piano).
5. DEBUSSY—Prélude *The Sunken Cathedral* (piano).

2

The Music of England in the Sixteenth, Seventeenth, and Eighteenth Centuries

One of England's many periods of greatness was marked by the reign of Queen Elizabeth (1559-1603) and so unique was this greatness that the appellation of Elizabethan evokes a series of pictures from the defeat of the Armada by a conglomeration of small privateers and warships to Shakespeare's, Marlowe's and Johnson's magnificent poetic utterances. This great vital spirit permeated another art—music, to an extent where it is a commonly accepted belief that the Elizabethan period represents Britain's greatest musical achievement.

THE PATTERNED VARIATION

Her composers were many and well-trained. They were the first to attempt to free the keyboard from its original subservient position, as an accompanist to other instruments or the voice. They seized upon vocal and instrumental models but used them in a unique manner to exploit a new and individual keyboard concept. This was no less than an attempt to justify the use of the keyboard for solo purposes and they found a perfect keyboard way to do so. They used the variation principle, which might have been inspired by a visit from Spain's most famous and blind organ composer, Cabezon, a composer of "Diferencias" or Differences, as the Spaniards called variations. But in adapting his favorite method of enlarging a composition, the Elizabethan composers, perhaps as a result of their flamboyant personalities, invented the idea of keyboard patterning. The virginalist's left hand would play the tune and his right hand would pit against it a group of notes in the shape of a specific rhythm. This rhythmic grouping would form a pattern. This pattern would be repeated consistently throughout the variation, beginning on higher or lower steps of the scale for the duration of the melody in the left hand. At the conclusion of the variation, another pattern, perhaps in the left hand now, would be adopted while the right hand played the same melody.

This is so well known now and accepted as a basic method of what is termed "motivic" writing that it is difficult for us to conceive it as not having always been known. But this patterned variation idea was new—it was truly indigenous to the keyboard, as the types of patterns adopted would not sound well on other instruments and would be awkward to play. It also gave these composers an idea of how to exploit the keyboard's potential and they made brilliant use of it. Many of their efforts, effective for their time, sound naïve and a bit primitive to our blasé twentieth-century ears.

MODALITY IN KEYBOARD WRITING

In the later renaissance and early Baroque period, the scales or keys used were not those which we familiarly know as major and minor. Rather, the predecessors of these later scales still prevailed and are called modes or "church" modes through their early use in plain-song or well-known church choral music. The use of these early scales resulted in chords and pitch changes strange to our ears and possessing the charm of the tastefully unusual. This modal usage by the virginalists adds one more beautiful attribute to their music; many of their chord progressions achieve a rich, varied, and lovely pattern of unaccustomed sound.

THE FANCY AND CONTRAPUNTAL WRITING

The prevailing technique of writing at this time was polyphonic or contrapuntal—that is, interwoven melodies. Since the church was such a natural center for music-making, many church chant tunes were well known. The composers uttered these on the keyboard and then proceeded to build contrapuntal compositions which were remote forerunners of the later German fugue. In this type of composition, termed a Fancy (for Fantasy), the cantus firmus, or church chant, was played alone as a single line of notes. Then it was repeated, starting some pitches higher or lower, while the original line of notes continued, providing a counter melody. The original melody might be taken up a third time by the introduction of a third line, again at a distance of some pitches from the second introduction, while the original two lines would weave two melodies now about the third. This method of introducing and reintroducing the cantus firmus would be continued at the composer's pleasure, with interludes minus the cantus firmus to relieve the monotony of hearing the theme too many times.

The purpose of this type of writing was to reveal another facet of the keyboard's potential, this time for contrapuntal performance. Only one other instrument could play this many melodies at once, the organ. Unlike the organ, the virginal was small enough to carry about; it had the attributes of both intimacy and light brilliance. It is not surprising, then, that its popularity with both composer-performer and audience was high.

THE POPULAR SONG THEMES

To further its popularity, the writing of variations on popular songs provided another avenue of usage. England was a singing country in those days. One has only to read Shakespeare to become aware of the many songs for every occasion. Titles as diverse as *The Carman's Whistle, The Woods So Wilde, The Leaves Be Greene,* provide an indication of the wide-ranging popular taste, nor is there any doubt that the populace knew and sang them by the hundreds. They were exquisitely harmonized by the Elizabethans.

THE CHARACTER PIECE

This was an age of aggressive individualism, to be matched only by nineteenth-century romanticism three hundred years later. These roistering, wenching, tippling, and quarreling Elizabethans were preoccupied with themselves and wrote the earliest "character" pieces under titles such as *"Dr. Bull's Myself."* They described themselves and their moods in music and thereby added another to the list of variety pieces which comprise a large portion of the literature through the centuries.

THE DANCES

In another category, music for the dance, they found a fertile field for their skill. The dances then prevalent were many—the sedate pavane (or peacock dance), the galliarde (a so-called leaping dance) with which it was usually paired, the one slow, the other fast; then the alman (or German dance), also sedate, and the coranto, much quicker, with which it might be paired. "Paired" means that the dancers would finish the first, wait a moment, and launch into the second. Besides these, there were dances like Volte (a very fast galliarde) and the Passamezzo or hastened pavane. There were Brawls (an English version of a French dance or Branle), native English Jigges and a series of dances so obscure to us now that we are puzzled as to their interpretation. Into this almost unknown category fall such dances as the Toye, the Muscadin, the Spagnioletta, and the Morisco.

To briefly recapitulate, the Elizabethan composers wrote almost everything that could be written for their tinkly, small but lightly brilliant instrument. They developed and exploited the patterned variation, they wrote quite complicated polyphonic works with themes like ecclesiastic melodies or hexachords (the first ascending six notes of our present-day major scale), they harmonized and varied popular songs, they conceived themselves as subjects for musical portraits and indulged in an orgy of dance composition. All of this took place over a period comprising some 70 years from the last half of the sixteenth century through almost the first third of the seventeenth century.

Figure 6. English Spinet (owned by Mr. B. C. Pritchard). (From James **Early Keyboard Instruments,** plate 31.)

THE FAMOUS COLLECTIONS

The major collections of keyboard music from this English period are as follows:

First, the famous *Fitzwilliam Virginal Book,* containing almost 300 pieces by more than 30 composers. Nearly all of them are English, with a sprinkling of composers from other lands. All the following collections contain some pieces already in the Fitzwilliam, which must be dated between 1613 and 1618.

Second, *My Ladye Nevells Book,* containing more than 30 keyboard compositions by one composer alone, William Byrd.

Third, *Benjamin Cosyn's Virginal Book,* date about 1600, containing almost 100 keyboard works.

Fourth, *Will Foster's Virginal Book,* 1624, containing about 70 keyboard works.

THE COMPOSERS

We must speak briefly of the best known Elizabethan composers. The oldest, and by many presumed the best, is William Byrd (1543-1623) who, like many musicians of his time, received most of his living from the court. He was one of England's greatest composers and his one hundred and twenty virginal compositions are masterpieces of their time. Byrd's taste is wonderfully refined and, compared to the other composers, he seems far more skilled as a musician.

Next in importance, and perhaps somewhat more important from the standpoint of keyboard writing, is Dr. John Bull (1563-1628). Like Byrd, he was a royal chapel musician; he lived a typically Elizabethan roistering existence, with something sufficiently dishonest about it to force him to flee to Flanders from whence he never dared return. His compositions for virginals, numbering about one hundred and fifty, while not nearly so notable for refinement as Byrd's, made up for their lack in two other ways. He was a virtuoso, a display artist, and wrote his pieces partly for this purpose. They are full of scale passages demanding exceptional digital speed, accuracy, and dexterity. They are as vigorous as the man must have been, with strong, driving rhythms. The other respect in which he is notable is in experimental writing. He uses key changes far more than his contemporaries.

Among many other composers, we might speak briefly of one more, Orlando Gibbons (1583-1625). His Fancies (or Fantasies) are purely written contrapuntal works and his popular song harmonizations and variations are masterworks for their time.

SUGGESTED PIECES FOR LISTENING

For those who would like to be introduced to the music of England by way of the virginal or harpsichord, an avenue of approach might be via the popular tune settings. *The Carman's Whistle* by Byrd is a delightful set of variations on an enchanting tune. His *The Bells* is an early and naïve but interesting bit of descriptive writing. The Earl of Salisbury Pavan shows his amazing invention in the new art of patterned variation writing. And any one of his many fantasias illustrates his mastery of the more academic and serious polyphonic art.

To continue this brief exploration of Britain's music, one should go to Bull's *The King's Hunt,* a somewhat obvious piece but full of Elizabethan vitality. His *John Bull's My Selfe, A Gigge,* and his *Dr. Bull's Juell* are two very short attempts at self-characterization, both rather simple for this great master of technical devices.

For others, Gibbons' *The Woods So Wilde,* a set of variations on an intricately harmonized tune, shows a late Elizabethan example of smooth sophistication in the development of the keyboard art by one of the very last of the great line of composers.

By way of contrast, Wm. Inglot's *The Leaves Be Greene* shows a simple setting of another tune with exquisite taste harmonically and a continued charming simplicity in the ensuing variations.

THE DECLINE OF THE KEYBOARD ART
IN THE SEVENTEETH CENTURY

By 1630, some twenty-seven years after the great queen's death, the Elizabethan effort was spent. Music for the keyboard continued to be written but it was insignificant. For many years England was in the musical doldrums and this listlessness was only temporarily and slightly relieved when composers like John Blow and his genius pupil, Henry Purcell, revived her greatness in music for the church, opera, and consorts of instruments, but alas, not for the keyboard. Some have attributed this decadence to the enervating effect on the arts to the reign of Oliver Cromwell, but this effect was short-lived. The monarchy was restored some twelve years later and once again a court was prepared to encourage and enjoy its artists. Not so, for the keyboard, its knell was more probably the wholesale transference of French and Italian developments in the keyboard suites (French) and many of the individual dances and preludes (Italian). The great art of the variation barely survived in the "ground," or obstinately repeated bass line. Too slavish imitation of foreign models without any indigenous injection caused the English keyboard music to suffer as all imitation suffers by weakening.

THE POST-ELIZABETHAN COMPOSERS

Blow (1649-1708), Purcell (1659-1695), Jeremiah Clarke (1674-1707), and William Croft (1678-1727) provide the best examplars of this weak and casual art. They wrote dances, preludes, grounds, some rounds (or more properly French rondeaux), and short, insignificant keyboard pieces. They put them into groups called Lessons or Ordres and used them for teaching. These keyboard efforts represented the smallest fraction of their total effort and their interest as a result is obviously minimal. Purcell's Lessons, written for teaching purposes, are not well organized. Each Lesson contains a prelude, an alman (in French Allemande) or German dance, a corrente (Italian dance), and sarabande (Spanish).

After this, the invasion and preemption of the musical scene in England by foreigners became well nigh complete in the eighteenth century. Handel, Domenico Scarlatti, Paradies and Alberti are among some of the names of composers active in England, but not English. Thomas Arne (1710-1778) was one of the few who strove to be a serious composer and we have some light sonatas by him which are replete with non-English and mainly Italianate ideas. No, England's keyboard day was done and as yet has not returned.

SUGGESTED READING

Apel, W. *Masters of the Keyboard*. Cambridge, Mass.: Harvard University Press, 1947, pp. 61-69 (Variations and Dances).

Bukofzer, M. *Music in the Baroque Era*. New York: W. W. Norton & Company, Inc., 1947, pp. 72, 73 (English Keyboard Music).

Kenyon, M. *Harpsichord Music*. London: Cassell and Company, Ltd., 1949, pp. 18-57 (The Virginals in England).

Loesser, A. *Men, Women and Pianos*. New York: Simon & Schuster, Inc., 1954, pp. 190-215 (Social history of the Virginals in England).

Naylor, E. W. *An Elizabethan Virginal Book*. New York: E. P. Dutton & Co., Inc., 1905, pp. 1-9 (Virginal Books).

Van Den Borren, C. *The Sources of Keyboard Music in England*, (translated by J. E. Matthew). London: Novello, 1913, pp. 1-6 (The instrument); pp. 29-52 (Keyboard Music in England, sixteenth-seventeeth centuries).

SUGGESTED WRITTEN ASSIGNMENTS

1. How did the Elizabethans change the use of the harpsichord?
2. What is the patterned variation principle?
3. How did they use the cantus firmus or plain chant on the virginals?

4. Name the kinds of music they wrote for the keyboard.
5. What are the major music collections of this period?
6. Who are the outstanding composers?
7. Why did keyboard writing decline in the late seventeenth century?
8. Who were the principal composers of the late seventeenth century?

SUGGESTED LISTENING

1. BULL—*In Nomine*
2. BULL—*My Selfe*
3. TOMKINS—*Fortune My Foe*
4. GIBBON—*The King's Juell*
5. BYRD—*The Earle of Salisbury*
6. BYRD—*The Bells*

SUGGESTED ADDITIONAL LISTENING

1. ANONYMOUS—*Oh, ye Happy Dames*
2. FARNABY—*Loth to Depart*
3. EDWARDS—*When Griping Griefs*
4. BYRD—*Ut, Re, Mi, Fa, Sol, La*
5. PURCELL—*A New Ground* (Variations)
6. ANONYMOUS—*Galliard*
7. ANONYMOUS—*My Lady Carey's Dompe*
8. PURCELL—*Suites*
9. PEERSON—*The Fall of the Leafe*
10. FARNABY—*A Toye*
11. MUNDAY—*Tres Partes in Una*
12. PURCELL—*Hornpipe*

Italy: Sixteenth-
Nineteenth Centuries

The Italians, like the English, approached the keyboard by way of the organ. Unlike the English, the Italians never drew a clear line between pieces written for the organ and those for the harpsichord. The words "ogni instrumenti" (any instrument which could encompass the written notes) were indeed placed on many manuscripts, but even if they were not so placed, it was implicit throughout the sixteenth and a part of the seventeenth century.

Unlike the English, the Italians never clearly differentiated between their organ and harpsichord (in Italian "cembalo") music. They rarely used the pedal board, which is a chromatic scale placed beneath the feet of the organist to aid in playing deep bass notes. So their music did not use the typical third staff of the German organist and was, therefore, indiscernible from harpsichord notation.

THE INTONAZIONE, THE PRELUDE, THE TOCCATA

In the days of the late renaissance of the sixteenth century, the fresh young keyboard art was partly impromptu—that is, it was improvised. During portions of the church service, when the choir was mute, the organist's fingers would wander over the keys, bridging the gap between choral offerings and preserving the religious atmosphere. These improvised interludes, finally becoming recognized as worthy of permanence on paper, were called Intonazione (Intonations) or pitch settings for the choir, and set in motion a kind of keyboard music which developed in two directions. In one, the later Prelude was born, the freest type of keyboard music imaginable, music of no rules except

that of brevity and usually music of one kind. That is to say, usually
a prelude was either slow or fast or moderate, but rarely both or all
three. The other of the two directions taken by the Intonazione was
that of a multi-sectioned keyboard piece, appropriately called the Toccata or touch piece, the "touch" referring to the fingertips on the
keyboard. The Toccata was a display piece and through its evolution
and later metamorphosis in the nineteenth century, it has always remained a piece written for the purpose of exploiting the keyboard's
potential. The number of sections could be as many or as few as desired; the early toccatas could run into a couple of dozen short sections of a few measures each. Its evolution during the next hundred
years gradually reduced the number of sections and made each one
longer until, by the eighteenth century, a toccata might have as few
as four quite long sections. The sections were not homogeneous in the
sense that there was only one theme and style. On the contrary, no
two sections were remotely alike. It was the composer's task to make
them as dissimilar as possible in order to illustrate the variety of usages
of the keyboard. The toccata generally began with a brilliant declamatory passage which might be followed by a few meditative, slow
(or "adagio") measures. Then a subjective recitative or colloquy type
of passage might ensue, followed by a sinuous chord progression.
This could break off and rapid interweaving scale passages might serve
as a forerunner to an intricate contrapuntal (or imitative in several
voice) passage.

THE CANZONE GROUP

In the early days of the Renaissance, two types of music were in
great demand. One was the French Chanson, or song, a piece to be
sung to a lute accompaniment and which was treated in a polyphonic
or imitative style. The other, in the church, was the motet, a very
serious Latin-text choral piece, also polyphonic. Oddly, these two
became two parts of a homogeneous grouping of keyboard pieces in
the early Baroque period called the canzone group, and consisting of
the canzone, the fantasia, the capriccio, and the ricercar. The last,
the ricercar, stemmed from the motet, while the fantasia and the
capriccio were slight variants of the canzone. The keyboard canzone
had begun as a transcription (or transference to the keyboard) of the
old vocal model. This group of keyboard pieces was also multi-sectioned
like the toccata and, in its early forms, had a different theme for each
section. Later, after the start of the seventeenth century, the theme
of each section was usually a variant of the first theme. The start

of the second section might consist of the first half alone of the main theme but elongated by making each note last twice as long as the original. This device is called augmentation. Or it might do the opposite, have many more notes than the original theme; the original theme might now form only the first half of the new section theme, this time greatly speeded by making each note only half as long as in the original statement. This device also has a name, diminution.

The pieces of the canzone group differed in another way from the toccata. Each section was imitative in what was later called fugal style, that is, the theme was stated alone, in solo fashion, then restated starting on another pitch, while a counter melody was played against it. Still a third entrance, perhaps at the distance of an octave, was made by the theme, while now two counter-melodies (or counterpoints) were heard as the first two lines of notes (called voices) continued to sound, making three simultaneous melodic lines in all. Interludes would be introduced between restatements of the theme and at the end of each section a complete stop (or cadence) would take place. In the following section, the altered theme would appear solo at first, followed by its reappearance in another voice and a counterpoint would be heard as in the previous section, but now this counter-melody would be utterly different from that in section one, thus providing contrast and unity at the same time (unity because of the theme reappearance though varied).

The canzones and capriccios were quite fast and somewhat gay, frequently exploiting a traditional rhythm like a drum rat-a-tat in their themes. The ricercar was traditionally slower and serious, being the descendant of the church motet.

Toward the end of the seventeenth century, the form died out and was replaced by the fugue, which was not too far removed from its prototype, starting with a solo theme, now generally longer than the canzone-type theme and more varied, and developing in a less sectional and more homogeneous style. Its greatest difference was in the injection of a new intense emotion which had been quite avoided in the older form. Usage of the new major and minor scales, considerable modulation or change of key procedures, and far greater usage of chromaticism or half-step progression were also incorporated into the new fugue setting.

THE VARIATIONS AND DANCES

One further compositional direction was of great use in exploring the keyboard possibilities. The composers of Italy, like those of England, delighted in writing variations, which they called partite, and tended to write so many on any one theme that they rarely expected any performer to play them all at one sitting.

Among the dances composed, the Italian equivalent to the English coranto or the French courante was very popular. This was the corrente, a rapid, light, perpetual motion dance, thinly written in just two voices and with a recurrent three-beat metre. Other dances were the pavane, passamezzo, forlana, siciliana, saltarello, etc., dances of varying speeds, rhythms, and metres. All the western world danced and each country had its native dances as well as its imports.

THE BAROQUE ERA

About the middle of the sixteenth century, a new attitude toward all art began to be felt in Italy and from there, because of Italy's constant communication with other countries, spread throughout the western world. The arts were expanding from an attitude of intimacy, either within the church or the courts, to an attitude ever grander, ever larger, and ever more ornamental. It was not a simple gloomy type of Gothic grandeur but rather an exuberant and highly detailed kind of massiveness which expressed itself in larger and more ornate complexity. In architecture, buildings were planned with larger rooms, higher ceilings, more light, and every inch of wall space, floors, ceilings, the roof-edges, and pillars were ornately decorated with carvings or paintings or marquetry.

In music, the intimate, subdued, and graceful conceptions of the renaissance were being enlarged, strengthened, made more aggressive, and highly involved. Opera or stage plays, set to music with musical utterance and supporting orchestras which grew constantly larger, came into being. Pieces for organ and cembalo were lengthened and made more idiomatic, exploiting the resources of both instruments as they had not been exploited heretofore.

The composers took pleasure in this new avenue of expression and began to experiment with two new kinds of scales which we now call major and minor. These new scales had one great advantage over the old church scales or modes. Using the new scales, the compositions they wrote could lengthen very much without becoming wandering or meandering in character, since in the new scales, the memory of and pull toward the final chord was so strong as not to be forgotten during the divagations of the piece and a great urge was always felt to eventually return to the final "do." The new scales had strikingly associated chord structures which helped to outline the new music clearly, and made the listener aware of where he was in the piece of music in relation to his original scale and final resting chord.

With these new scale (or key) and chord entities, the compositions took on a richer, more varied quality. The toccatas grew more complicated, their scale passages more intricate, longer, and more brilliant, their chords richer with sliding chromatic passing (or bridge) notes, their imitative passages more involved, their recitatives more subjective and intensely descriptive.

The art was at its height in the first third of the seventeenth century, but, like all human endeavor, it began to recede as after a high tide and, by the middle of the seventeenth century, had deteriorated, while a new style began to germinate in the ashes of the old.

THE BINARY SONATA, THE CHURCH SONATA

This new style envisaged a virtual emasculation of the old serious contrapuntal writing and its replacement by a light two-voiced, short and highly varied show piece. It was made in approximately two equal parts, now called binary form, and was much shorter than any of the former favorites like the canzone group. It was nonimitative. It used the new scales of major and minor, thus becoming what was finally termed "tonal." It was extremely compact, crowding into two short halves a variety of rhythms and even complete short melodies. It followed a general rule of modulation or change of scale (or key) going from one key to that five tones higher at the end of the first half, then starting in the new key and returning to the original at the close. Sometimes it began in the minor scale, went to a closely related major key instead of five notes higher, and then made the customary return.

This new piece was simply termed "Sonata" and, small as it was, became a fine art product, so full of beauty that today it is valued quite as highly as pieces twenty times its length and many times more grandiose. Along with this, and keeping pace with the sonata, was a type of suite or group of pieces, oddly bearing the title of church sonata, or "sonata da chiesa," having nothing to do with religion but so designated to deny any dance origin. This group of pieces had the order of slow, fast, slow, fast, four in number. The classic sonata, the symphony, the instrumental combinations of trio, quartet, and quintet, all derived at least partly from this small and quite modest keyboard source.

THE COMPOSERS

A discussion, however brief, of the composers of Italy must include some who were not necessarily great but were credited with either originating or developing the pieces we have been describing. The *Intonazione* has been waveringly traced to Merulo (1533-1604). Two Gabrieli's, uncle and nephew, Andrea (1510-1586) and Giovanni (1557-1612), are credited with aiding greatly in its development on the organ only. But it was Frescobaldi (1583-1643), organist and cembalist, who composed the toccatas and preludes which derived from the now dissolved Intonazione and made them pieces of surpassing beauty. He also composed many pieces in the canzone group style and was quite as famous for his variation writing, called partite in Italian. To him, also, we are indebted for something almost as priceless as his pieces, namely, directions for conceiving them musically and details in their performance. From him we learn that the improvisational aspect of the writing must be fulfilled in tempo (speed) by the performer, that he must begin a toccata at a slower tempo than he will later pursue, that he must be prepared to be very flexible in the performance of music, ornamenting it in the famous Italian florid and improvised style, playing trills as long or longer than the written notes might indicate, that in the partite (variations) he should not cavil at breaking off whenever he thinks the listeners have had enough, even if the piece contains many unplayed sections. In short, the Italian music was highly expressive, not at all rigid, and its performance was expected to reveal a large measure of the performer's own taste.

Frescobaldi served the cause of music in still another way. Younger composers of his and another country, Germany, came to study with him and carried home with them a wealth of the great master's ideas and disciplines.

Two Scarlattis come into our history. Only one is most pertinent to our purpose. They are father and son, Alessandro (1660-1725), and Domenico (1685-1757). Alessandro assumes little importance, though he was a great opera composer, but the same cannot be said for his keyboard efforts. We find it difficult to account for the origins of the fantastic versatility of the younger Scarlatti. Not only was he original, but his genius was so fecund that he composed over 600 short binary form sonatas for the cembalo. An overwhelming number deserve the appellation of wonderful works of art. They are miniature by comparison with our greatly grown sonatas but are a treasure of marvels. He exploits the resources of the instrument rhythmically, tonally, and melodically. He offers the harpsichord performer the opportunity to display his ability as not even the greatest of the Elizabethan virginalists, John Bull, ever dreamed of doing. And the manifold beauties revealed in his many sonatas are so overwhelming that even their transference to the later keyboard of the pianoforte does them no damage, something which cannot be said for the early English and French music, which suffers greatly in the transferral.

A brief catalogue of the technical devices used by Scarlatti provides a compendium of most of the techniques subsequently rediscovered and practiced by pianists today. In his many hundred sonatas are to be found fast and far leaps, crossed hands, double notes played at a furious rate, double trills, broken octaves, and rapidly repeated tones, to name a few of his many devices. His long sojourn in Spain, where he was employed at the royal court, brought him inevitably into contact with the Spanish musical art, both of folk origin and the more cultivated types. In his music are easily traced the melodic intervals of Spanish music, the imitations of their dance rhythms, and the castanet and vihuela (lute) strumming sounds.

He also delighted in a kind of dissonance called a crush (or acciaccatura). It is represented by a chord inclusive of its neighbor notes. Those many dissonant notes sounded simultaneously in a surrounding atmosphere of pure consonance give the music a bite and color which can be termed the intrusion of brute force into a milieu of delicacy.

For the keyboard, then, Frescobaldi and Domenico Scarlatti are Italy's greatest composers.

Names like Durante (1684-1755), Zipoli (1688-1726), Galuppi (1706-1785), Cimarosa (1749-1801), and Grazioli (1746-1820) fill out the picture of an Italian art which, while not dying, was revealing a loss of keyboard interest. Platti (1690-1762) wrote sonatas in a style strikingly revealing of future trends. Their four movements alternating slow and fast tempi are in the earliest preclassic tradition with evenly balanced phrases and using short motivic groups of notes combined into larger phrase entities. Galuppi and Cimarosa show similar traits. Their writing is thin, and leans ever more toward simple harmonic progressions with melodies superimposed in the new preclassic style. Grazioli, thought to be the last of the harpsichord composers, wrote a kind of pre-Mozart type of piano sonata in three movements, fast, slow, fast, but sadly wrote them even after Mozart's death, clinging to an early classic style even while Beethoven was thunderously changing the entire concept of keyboard composition.

The nineteenth century saw the complete cessation of Italian interest in the keyboard. The love of opera wiped out all other interests and it was and is a fact that to this day, keyboard music's role has been minor in the Italian musical art.

Suggested Reading

Bukofzer, M. *Music in the Baroque Era.* New York: W. W. Norton & Company, Inc., 1947. pp. 45-50. (Early Baroque dances, variations, toccata, intonazione, prelude, and fugal forms.)

Dart, T. *The Interpretation of Music.* London: Hutchinson's Universal Library, 1954, pp. 103-132, (style).

Dolmetsch, A. *The Interpretation of the Music of the 17th and 18th Centuries.* London: Novello & Co., Ltd., 1946, pp. 4-8. (Frescobaldi's instructions for the performance of his music.)

Gillespie, J. *Five Centuries of Keyboard Music.* Belmont, California: Wadsworth Publishing Co., Inc., 1965, pp. 62-79. (Italian cembalo music.)

Kenyon, M. *Harpsichord Music.* London, Cassell and Company, Ltd., 1949, pp. 112-130. (The composers and music of Italy in the 17th and 18th centuries.)

Kirby, F. E. *A Short History of Keyboard Music.* New York: The Macmillan Co., 1966, pp. 64-79, (Frescobaldi and others); pp. 160-166, (D. Scarlatti).

Kirkpatrick, R. *Domenico Scarlatti,* Princeton University Press: 1953. (A fine and definitive biography.)

Suggested Written Assignments

1. How did the Intonazione come into existence?
2. What two types of keyboard composition derived from the Intonazione?
3. Describe the character of each of these two types.
4. What is a "church" sonata? How many movements has the church sonata, and what is the order of their tempi?
5. Four types of keyboard pieces are included in the Canzone group. What are they; from whence are they derived, and what do they all have in common?
6. What did the Canzone group evolve into, and how did its successor differ from the Canzone group?
7. What style of keyboard writing was practiced by Domenico Scarlatti? What is virtuosity and how did he display it in his music?
8. What happened to Italian keyboard music in the nineteenth century?

Suggested Listening

1. Frescobaldi—*Capriccio sopra un Soggetto*
2. Frescobaldi—*Three Galliards*
3. D. Scarlatti—Sonata in B♭ (Longo 498)
4. A. Scarlatti—Toccatas
5. B. Pasquini—Canzona

Suggested Additional Listening

1. Zipoli—Harpsichord Suites
2. Galuppi—Sonatas Nos. 4 and 5
3. Platti—Sonata in D
4. Grazioli—Sonata in B♭

5. D. SCARLATTI—Sonatas for Harpsichord (Longo 385, 387)
6. RUTINI—Andante
7. MARTINI—Allegro
8. MATIELLI—Adagio
9. FRESCOBALDI—Four Correnti
10. FRESCOBALDI—*Canzone primo, seconda, quarta*
11. FRESCOBALDI—*Partite Sopra L'Aria de Ruggiero*

4

France: Sixteenth-
Eighteenth Centuries;
Spain; Netherlands

We think of the French character as being one with a love of precision, exquisite taste, a love for the dance, somewhat cynical, with refined wit, a detestation of vulgarity, urbane good manners, and gallantry toward women. Their art bears this out.

In Chapter 1, reference is made to the lute attainment in France. Two brothers, named Gaultier, brought this instrument's technique and composition to such a pitch that they actually motivated its decline, since no one felt able to rise beyond their zenith. We do not know all the influences which acted upon the lutenists (lute composers and performers), but we do know that they probably received ideas from across the channel where the Elizabethan composers were boldly experimenting. They may have received ideas for ornamentation and patterned figure variations from that source. On the other hand, in ornamentation, the shoe may have been on the other foot. Ornaments first became codified by the lutenists, and France's first outstanding harpsichord composer is said to have adapted seven of the eight most common ornaments to the newly popularized clavecin.

THE LUTE SUITE; THE HARPSICHORD SUITE

In the late renaissance and early Baroque periods, it was the most ordinary thing to transfer a piece of music from the voice to the lute, from the lute to the harpsichord, from the harpsichord to a group of string players, and so on. When the clavecin began to supersede the lute in French favor, it was only natural that not only would the music of the lute be transferred or, as it is called in musical terminology, transcribed, but all the ornaments and many other ideas, such as writing suites in one key, would be automatically incorporated into the new instrument's literature. The lute suite and the clavecin suite would have been even more alike, even identical, if the composers had not been made aware that they could write many more notes to be played by two hands on the harpsichord than could be played by only one hand on the lute. So the harpsichord (or clavecin) suite was an expanded lute suite and could contain, as did the lute suite, anywhere up to twenty or more pieces in the same key.

These pieces were mainly dances. France was a dancing nation and the indigenous dances were included with the imported ones. The "basse danse" was in slow tempo. The "allemande," or so-called German dance, was smooth and gliding. The "courante" was full of odd rhythms and was danced crosswise from corner to corner of a room. The "gavotte" and "branle" were rather stilted but possessed of charm. The "rigaudon" was very lively. These and many others were joined with gigues from England, "sarabandes" from Spain, "pavanes" from Italy, etc.

THE RONDEAU; THE VARIATIONS

The French did not stop with stuffing their suites with dances. They also inserted "rondeaux" or what has been vulgarly described as the "musical club sandwich." The main melody may be compared with the layers of bread since it recurs several times. The principal melody is relieved and contrasted with alternate melodies termed "couplets" which would correspond to the filling between the various bread layers.

Then the French also wrote the ubiquitous variation type of piece prevalent, as we already know, in England and Italy. But their variation structure was somewhat different. In England the composers had recourse to their innovation, the patterned variation. The Italian type was freer, more florid and less repetitive in its use of patterns. The French organized the variations by note value change, a kind of rhythmic diminution. The first variation following the theme statement might be in consecutive eighth notes, two to each beat in a kind of perpetual motion arrangement. The second variation might shorten the note values to triplet eighths in which the same steady beat would now be divided into three equal parts. The third variation might see the perpetual motion pattern made up of four equal notes to each beat, or four-sixteenths. Though the beat might be unvarying, the effect would be one of speeding up in each variation. This way of conceiving successive variations, or "doubles" as they were termed, was important for the future of the variation, for as late as Mozart, this style of writing the first several variations prevailed and thus what was begun in French harpsichord music in the mid-seventeenth century found its descendants in the pianoforte music of latter eighteenth century Germany.

THE PRÉLUDE, TOMBEAU, AND STYLE BRISÉ

The French also wrote préludes, but here again their concept represented an interesting departure from the English and Italian types. The lutenists took great pride in their creativity, and the art of improvisation or composing on the spur of the moment was carried out to a remarkable degree. In their préludes, they went so far as to write the pitches on the staff, but they wrote the notes without relative values— that is to say, all the notes were written conventionally as whole (four quarter beat) notes, without bar lines. To a musician of today, this would be a dismaying sight, like a painting in one color only, and the realization of these notes, to be endowed with relative values in half, quarter, eighth or sixteenth note values, would be like trying to sort out and apply appropriate shades of color to the monochromatic painting. This prélude, as with most of the other lute creations, was transferred to the clavecin.

A peculiarly French concept of graciousness lay in still another of their compositions. This was the Tombeau, literally a tomb piece, a kind of musical monument, dedicated to one recently deceased who might be considered immortalized in music. These pieces were conventionally slow and, oddly, usually took the shape of the allemande, but very slowed. There was a reason for the choice of allemande to represent this type of death tribute. The allemande was smooth and flowing, achieving a kind of suave perpetual motion through still another lute-derived device. This was known as free voicing and represented a way of disguising the lute's inability to sustain simultaneously two or three lines of music. A clever deception was perpetrated by hearing one line arrive at a held or long-valued note, and while that note was sustained, another line would be heard above or below the first. In the hands of an able lutenist, the illusion of two interdependent lines approaching and receding from each other with an occasional and short-lasting duet of simultaneous sounds was most convincing. This occasioned another transferral to the keyboard and its perpetuation was assured since no allemande could be clearly identified as such without these stylistic attributes.

One other lute habit persisted after its demise. This was called "style brisé" or broken-voiced style and consisted simply of the slow arpeggiation of chords, that is, the playing of the notes of the chord consecutively rather than simultaneously. This "breaking" of the chord, particularly at the ends of sections and the terminal chords of the piece, or cadences, persisted into the eighteenth century, long after the lute had become almost a curiosity.

The French also pioneered the use of the new major and minor scales, turning quite completely away from the old modes without the backward glances and reluctance shown by the Italians, the English, and the Germans, all of whom tended to write for a space with a somewhat confusing mixture of the old and the new.

THE CHARACTER PIECE

The English had probably been the first to write "character" pieces. This idea was seized upon by the French, and in their sophisticated manner, enlarged and refined. Thus, composers would write portraits in sound of all the members of their family, their aristocratic patrons, towns they felt they could characterize, scenes, especially of nature, in which the calls of birds, the lowing of kine, clucking of chickens, etc., would be sedulously imitated, and sound such as a mill might make with the water chuckling about the immersed mill wheel, the plangent ring of hammers on metal, etc., would all be included. It is small wonder that the clavecin became a king of instruments when it afforded so many opportunities for exploitation.

ROCOCO STYLE

In their quest, whether conscious or otherwise, for a kind of music which would best mirror the French spirit of the seventeenth century, the composers began quite early to use the "serious" style (imitative or polyphonic) with a degree of reserve, and showed an early tendency to write with increasing emphasis on a melody which might stand almost alone, unimitated, and supported by small uttered chords or a broken chord in simple rhythm as a bass. This emphasis on melody and harmonic support without counterpoint came to have the overall name of homophony in later times. Also, they began to favor a kind of simple balance in the phrase length of the melody, making the phrase two or four bars in length and avoiding the former spinning out by the use of motivic writing so dear to the contrapuntalists. This tendency toward simplicity in melody, simplicity in accompaniment, simplicity in phrase length, and one thing more, an ever-increasing abundance or a kind of ornamental profusion so that the melody at times was scarcely recognizable, so smothered was it in turns and trills, finally changed the course of music. It began to show an effeteness, a preciousness which avoided the dramatic and profound but stressed the tender, shallow, and superficial, the "pretty" side of music. This was a kind of music saying very little but saying it with ineffable grace. It has received the name of "rococo" from the French "rocaille" or shell, and refers to the use of the shell in ornamental decoration.

The rococo style in faience (china), furniture, in the concept of graceful miniaturization, as illustrated in the seventeenth and eighteenth century French gardens, set in motion a force in music which, allied with the Italian keyboard style of Domenico Scarlatti and his contemporaries, was to result, through the development of this "style gallant" as it was called in Germany, in the monumental "classic" style of the latter half of the eighteenth century. The gentle, highly-stylized and tinkly tunes of the rococo with their constant and graceful ornaments are a far cry from the great classic sonatas of Mozart and Beethoven, but the form in which the latter are cast owes much to this earliest effort to avoid the consequences of the serious polyphonic style.

THE COMPOSERS

The keyboard development in France was set in motion by Chambonnières (1602-1672). He left two collections, mainly of dance music, and while he used the polyphonic style, he used it with a kind of spareness which already pointed the way to its ultimate decline. His use of ornaments is already quite profuse, and he shows, in his sectional and final cadences, the strong lute tradition of broken-voiced style which endures in dance endings well into the eighteenth century both in France and Germany.

His fame is further enhanced by his sponsorship and presumably his teaching of the first composer of an illustrious family of musicians, Louis Couperin (1626-1661). His music is very dignified, tends to lie in the lower registers of the clavecin, and rarely uses many short valued notes as if they might be frivolous.

Another of Chambonnières' pupils and his successor at the King's court was d'Anglebert (1628-1691). He is historically most famous for preceding his printed collection of music with a table of codified ornaments—29 of them. With this imposing number, it should not surprise us to note that his pieces are inundated with ornaments, the perform-ance of which demands arduous study.

There then occurs a substantial list of composers advancing the keyboard art by enlarging and solidifying the key and chord structure and building on the foundations laid down by Chambonnières and Louis Couperin. Marchand (1669-1732), Clérambault (1676-1749), and Le Roux (died after 1705) are in the main stream. Collections by them and various others are available. The last named, Le Roux, is believed to have provided the greatest of all composers, Johann Sebastian Bach, with thematic and stylistic material for some pieces in his suites.

At the zenith of the keyboard art, possibly the greatest French com-poser appeared. He was François Couperin, (1668-1733), called Le Grand or the great, a nephew of Louis Couperin and a scion of this very musical family. He brought the art to its highest French peak and though he was followed by notable composers, it is undoubtedly to him that most musicians refer when they speak of the great clave-cinists. He called his great collection of suites "ordres" and they repre-sent a meticulous ordering of the best in his great art. The pieces in each ordre range from the stylized dances, allemandes, courantes, sarabandes and gigues, to personalized tone portraits of people, nature descriptions, legends, satires and anecdotes. His ordres are longer in many cases than the conventional length and, unlike the earlier lute-affected groupings, the pieces in an ordre are not all in the same key.

He brought to the art a fervid imagination which found an infini-tude of outlets in rhythms, harmonies, melodies, forms, and ornaments. His exploitation of the clavecin's resources is far greater than his pre-decessors and successors achieved and his music ran a universal gamut of emotion. In his desire as teacher as well as composer to have his works properly performed, he wrote a most comprehensive treatise on the performance aspects of his music, entitled "The Art of Playing the Clavecin." His description of ornament performance is sufficiently com-plicated to make the aspiring harpsichordist aware of the profundity of this aspect of performance. His awareness of touch and tone brings home to the reader an appreciation of the sensitivity of the seventeenth century musical ear and the sophisticated musical demands already made at this early date. His explanations of rhythmic subtleties, too delicate to be notated but nevertheless expected in performance, is another revelation of the heights to which the performing art had ascend-ed at this time.

One would hardly expect France to produce two such composers and if Rameau (1683-1764) did not, perhaps, achieve the universality

Figure 7. "Empress" Harpsichord, one of the largest, made by John Broadwood for Maria Theresa, dated 1773. (From Hipkins **Musical Instruments,** plate 33.) (South Kensington Music Loan Collection, 1883.)

of expression on the clavecin that Couperin did, he ran a close second in other respects. He was not quite as dedicated to the keyboard, since he was primarily an opera composer, as he was also an organist and, above all, France's greatest theorist. But his three clavecin collections almost rival, if they do not quite equal, Couperin's in their scope and variety. Unlike Couperin, he achieves an austerity and purity of expression which Couperin offsets by his delightful and subtle colorations. They both wrote inimitible descriptive music. Rameau's *The Hen* has a raucously realistic imitation of cock-crowing and his *Recall of the Birds* is alive with bird song. Since he lived after Couperin, some of his works begin to reveal futuristic aspects; pieces like *The*

Cyclops in three distinct sections and two themes presage the sonata-allegro form, which later, in another country (Germany), set a seal upon formal development.

After Rameau, the French clavecinists began to recede from the high water mark of musical art; composers like Dandrieu (1682-1740), Daquin (1694-1772), Dagincourt or d'Agincourt (1684-1758), and Duphly (1715-1789) continued the tradition, but could offer nothing substantially new or as great as what they found. Daquin's *The Cuckoo* is only an echo of Rameau's *The Hen* and not the best echo. The French keyboard art at this time practically disappeared and made its reappearance when, in the nineteenth century, the predecessors of that subtle offspring of Romanticism, Impressionism, began to discover in the clavecin's successor, the piano, a whole new realm of tonal and emotional possibilities.

SPAIN 1550-1780

The peripheral countries of Europe in the sixteenth-eighteenth centuries, Spain, Portugal and Belgium, were understandably less progressive than what we might term the main stem countries, England, Italy, France, and Germany.

In the sixteenth century, Spain was still a power with considerable if declining vitality and it produced a blind organist and composer, Antonio Cabezón (1510-1566), who, it is thought, gave impetus to the Elizabethans of England when, with other musicians in 1554, he visited that country in the retinue of his monarch. In an early chapter of this work, mention is made of the belief that Cabezón may have planted the seed in the minds and ears of the English which led to their great contribution to the keyboard, the patterned variation. Cabezón wrote "diferencias" or differences, the Spanish term for variations. He wrote for the lute (vihuela in Spanish) and for "keyed" instruments, not discriminating in the kinds of keyed instruments.

Spain's sole remaining claim to a composer of fame before her musical renaissance at the end of the nineteenth century is Padre Antonio Soler (1729-1783). A modest, self-effacing monk of the famed Escorial monastery, he wrote prodigiously and included at least 130 harpsichord sonatas as a relatively small part of his catalog of compositions. He was, we know, a pupil of Domenico Scarlatti; his works resemble those of his master. Though they have an uneven charm, vitality and fluency, they fall short of the superior genius so consistently exhibited in the writing of D. Scarlatti. They are superficially similar, in bipartite or two-halved form. Like Scarlatti, he uses several themes in each sonata, stringing them together with far less deftness than his teacher. He leans heavily on harmony as a basis for his melodies, and indulges in surprisingly frequent modulation so that one sonata contains excerpts in many keys. This is not usually a successful contribution to the work as a whole and shows a restlessness and perhaps an inability to control his musical material; viewed from another viewpoint, it may perhaps be a compulsion toward innovation. Despite these drawbacks, one can find an occasional gem in his sonatas that is relatively flawless and well worth hearing. Like Scarlatti, he transferred well to the modern piano keyboard and deserves the attention of performers and students.

NETHERLANDS

In the Netherlands, one figure stands out, not because of his works for harpsichord, since he was primarily an organist and called "a maker of organists," but because he became a kind of focal point to attract English composers, German, and, we believe without direct evidence, some Italians. He was Jan Sweelinck (1562-1621), so highly regarded in England that four of his works appear in the famous Fitzwilliam Virginal Collection. In his organ works, the English influence and the Italian are evident, the English in his complex and voluminous variations, the Italian in his toccatas and fantasias. Being an organist, he associated the great body of his work with the church, but there are important secular compositions like his variations on popular songs, similar to and perhaps derived from English models.

When the French came into prominence in the seventeenth century, their influence was not much felt to the south in Spain, but from this time, the Netherlands came under their sway. The Belgian composers wrote French music with a certain genuflection in the direction of Germany. The old English influence was still present, so that by the eighteenth century, the Belgians were writing a rather charming and virile mixture, mainly French in its orientation but with enough of German and English to make their music simpler, less ornamented (though still sufficiently embellished for their taste), highly rhythmic and extremely tuneful.

At least four composers represent this last flowering of the Baroque in eighteenth century Belgium. Chief among them and Belgium's pride is Jean-Baptiste Loeillet (1680-1730). About five years older than J. S. Bach, he wrote suites that superficially resemble his noble contemporary in the order of their dances, but his gigues reflect a strong English type of drive and length. The suites follow the German-ordained pattern of dances. They are also German in their flavorful mingling of Italian Correntes with French and English dance styles, as mentioned above.

One of the most talented Belgian composers whose fame is diminished by his slight surviving production is Josse Boutmy (1697-1779). A very few complete dance suites and fragments of a few more are his present legacy. The suites are far more French in style than are Loeillet's. One, undoubtedly the finest, is most descriptive. The first movement depicts the sounds of war, characterized mainly by a conventional "galloping horse" rhythm and trumpet calls. Other movements are in the "portrait" class, so familiar in Couperin. The gigue with which this suite closes is very English in its driving triplet rhythm and French in its imitative devices. The melodies of all the movements are fresh and naïve, exhibiting a constant and charming taste.

It is clear that these musical border countries were followers and not leaders in the art. They all loved music and made music; they mirrored the great movements in the art which eddied about them and produced great composers, but their contribution was more for themselves and their own time than for the world and posterity.

Suggested Reading

Bukofzer, M. *Music in the Baroque Era*. New York: W. W. Norton & Company, Inc., 1947, pp. 164-172 (lute and harpsichord music and composers of the middle Baroque); pp. 251-253 (late Baroque).

Chase, G. *The Music of Spain*. New York: Dover Publications, Inc., 1959, pp. 114-116 (Soler).

Gillespie, J. *Five Centuries of Keyboard Music*: Belmont, Calif.: Wadsworth Publishing Co., Inc., 1965, pp. 80-99 (French clavecinists); pp. 103-105 (Netherlands composers); pp. 111-113 (Spain).

Grout, D. J. *A History of Western Music*. New York: W. W. Norton & Company, Inc., 1960, pp. 347-349 (Suite dances).

Harich-Schneider, E. *The Harpsichord*. Kassel: Barenreiter, 1954. pp. 30-44 (Ornamentation).

Jean-Aubry, G. *An Introduction to French Music*. London: Palmer and Hayward, 1917.

Kenyon, M. *Harpsichord Music*. London: Kassel and Co., 1949, pp. 72-76 (French composers); pp. 80-89 (their music).

Kirby, F. E. *A Short History of Keyboard Music*. New York: The Free Press, 1966, pp. 79-83 (clavecin composers and their music); pp. 154-159 (F. Couperin and Rameau).

Landowska, W. *Landowska on Music*, (translated by D. Restout, asst. R. Hawkins). New York: Stein & Day, Publishers, 1965, pp. 256-279 (French composers).

Lang, P. H. *Music in Western Civilization*. New York: W. W. Norton & Company, Inc., 1941, pp. 385-387 (seventeenth-century French music); pp. 541-543 (late baroque).

Rubio, Father S. *Introduction to the Sonatas of Father Soler*. Madrid: Union Musical Española, 1957.

SUGGESTED WRITTEN ASSIGNMENTS

1. What were the French innovations in keyboard music?
2. How did the French suite or ordre come into being?
3. The serious or polyphonic style was changed into what kind of music in France?
4. How did the ornaments come to be organized into tables and why was this done by the French?
5. What is meant by the terms rondeau, tombeau, rococo?
6. Besides dances, what other forms of keyboard writing were practiced by François Couperin and Rameau?
7. What kind of composing led ultimately to the classic style in Germany?
8. When this era ended, what happened to French composition? When did it achieve its next advance?
9. What foreign composer had the most profound influence on Spanish baroque music and how did this come about?
10. What influences were felt in Belgium and from whence did they spring?

SUGGESTED LISTENING

1. CHAMBONNIÈRES—*Sarabande, Drollerie, Allemande dit L'Affligée, Volte*
2. LULLY—Courante
3. LOEILLET—Gigue from G Minor Suite
4. L. COUPERIN—Chaconne in D Minor
5. F. COUPERIN—*Rigaudon en Rondeau* (Vendangeuses)

SUGGESTED ADDITIONAL LISTENING

1. F. COUPERIN—Eighth Ordre (Suite)
2. F. COUPERIN—Chaconne *La Favorite*
3. L. COUPERIN—*Branle de Basque, Pavanne, Pasacaille*
4. RAMEAU—*Les Cyclops*
5. RAMEAU—*Le Rappel des Oiseaux*
6. RAMEAU—Suite, A Minor
7. ZWEELINCK—Variations
8. CABEZÓN—Diferencias Sobre *La Gallarda Milanesa*
9. CABANILLES—*Tiento de Falsas*
10. PADRE SOLER—Sonatas
11. NEBRA—Sonata

Germany:
Mid-Seventeenth through
Mid-Eighteenth Centuries

INTERNATIONALISM

From the beginning of keyboard music in Germany, we are presented with a phenomenon that has remained the perquisite of that country until the twentieth century, when all countries of the western world adopted its musical attitude. This may be termed musical internationalism. In Germany a custom arose of study abroad or, failing that, of voluminous perusal of foreign music brought to Germany. So large was this foreign influence that from the early part of the seventeenth century, Germany was "snowed under" with Italian, French, and, to a small extent, English music styles. The Germanic composers prided themselves more on writing in other countries' styles than in developing their own and, indeed, it was not until the period following the great J. S. Bach that the tables began to turn and other countries began to follow Germany's lead.

Germany's awakening to the keyboard came via Sweelinck and the organ in the Netherlands in one direction, via Italy and the harpsichord-cum-organ from the south through Vienna, and via France and the harpsichord through Paris.

FROBERGER: TOCCATAS AND SUITES

The true harpsichord composers were to be found toward the middle of the seventeenth century in Vienna where the court musicians, so close to Italy and France, wrote music which complimented their foreign masters. The first and one of the greatest was Johann Jacob Froberger (1616-1667), whose life had a nomadic, almost picaresque flavor. He was a true Teutonic composer, in that he went to Italy and subsequently wrote toccatas with all the flavor of their Italian models plus a broadening, dramatic continuity of musical content which marked them as works of a German. Then he went on a further musical quest, landing in England. He then visited France and finally returned to Vienna with his treasury of compositions greatly enriched with the styles of two more countries.

His toccatas are probably for organ but are so rich harmonically and so varied in keyboard devices that they are effective not only on the harpsichord but even on the pianoforte, an instrument still to be invented. Modeling on the toccatas of the great Frescobaldi, he reduces the excessive number of sections, which even Frescobaldi suggested might be done, enlarges the smaller number of sections which remain, reveals still further advances in the techniques of the keyboard, and imbues them with a well-nigh fiery vitality.

These toccatas are still organ oriented. When Froberger turned to the harpsichord, he showed the results of his French sojourn, for he took the multimovement French Ordre (or suite) and, with Teutonic logic, proceeded after an experimental period, to set it in order, beginning always with an allemande, following it with a courante in French style, placing a gigue next (of English origin), and concluding with a sarabande or slow Spanish dance. On his death, his widow rearranged the order, transposing the sarabande and gigue to make a more effective conclusion, and this order of dances, allemande, courante, sarabande, and gigue remained the prototype of the German harpsichord suite for over 100 years. This is not to say that all composers followed this order. J. S. Bach did, and since we happily associate him with the German Baroque suite, we feel that Froberger pointed the way to Bach's great satisfaction.

Despite their importance to history, Froberger's harpsichord works are not sufficiently sophisticated to merit performance today. The work of his great successors has relegated Froberger to an honored place only in history, not in the concert hall.

KUHNAU: THE BIBLICAL SONATAS

Our history of keyboard music contains anomalies in the form of concentrated mention of compositions which are of undoubted historic importance without necessarily being beautiful. Into this category fall the suites of Froberger, slight pieces in themselves but important in what they portended. The same may be said for the suites of Georg Bohm (1661-1733) since we presume J. S. Bach was influenced by them as well as by Froberger. Above all, this doubtful accolade may also be bestowed on the six Biblical Sonatas of Johann Kuhnau (1660-1722), Bach's immediate predecessor as cantor of the famous St. Thomas church in Leipzig. These multi-movement works have an extramusical commentary, based on biblical history from the battle between David and Goliath through Jacob's death and burial. The lengthy and explicit commentary provided by the composer made the purpose of each musical excerpt crystal clear, and it is perhaps a point for us to remember that devotees found music as hard to comprehend then as now. How else, otherwise, can we explain the enormous popularity enjoyed by this obviously inferior music with its dull repetitive rhythm patterns, its monotonous harmonies, its naïve use of devices like a rapid scale passage to signify the flight of David's slung stone and Goliath crumbling to earth via short chromatic descending figures.

Figure 8. Bound Clavichord, containing fewer strings than keys, in the Reichsmuseum, Amsterdam. (From F. J. Hirt's **Meisterwerke des Klavierbaus,** p. 312, 1955.)

GOTTLIEB MUFFAT: THE SUITES

The judgment of history is not always accurate. One of its mistakes is the neglect acorded to the Componimenti Musicali of Gottlieb Muffat (1690-1770). These musical compositions comprise six fine suites and a chaconne. Muffat suffered two disadvantages. A Viennese, he had the misfortune to be only five years the junior of J. S. Bach and posterity has seen most of Bach's German contemporaries overshadowed to the point of oblivion by his magnificence. Then, too, Gottlieb Muffat was the son of a then famous composer, Georg Muffat. Because of his father's studies in France, he was very heavily influenced by French style. His most beautiful d minor suite begins with a French overture; the allemande and courante which follow are intricately laced with all manner of ornamentation. Only a greater rhythmic solidity and a thicker texture in all but the two charming minuets mark his German heritage. The combination is quite as felicitous as Bach's, and it remains only for some enterprising harpsichordist of note to bring them to public notice and acclaim.

HANDEL

It is a surprise and disappointment that one of the two greatest German composers, George Frederick Handel (1685-1759), born in the same year as Bach, did not write more or better keyboard compositions than his suites, variations, and a considerable number of miscellaneous pieces. His keyboard works do not illustrate his genius any more than do Purcell's suites. The reason may have been in his relatively slight interest in the medium. The eight principal suites are not well balanced, some movements being three to four times the length of others and too long for their own musical worth. His facile technique is always evident, as is his abundant imaginative variety, but there is evident a carelessness evinced not only as already indicated but also in a superfluity of ideas and a hodge-podge of styles, German in their contrapuntal intricacy, French in their abundant ornamentation, and Italian in their divisions (written-out florid passages) and in their fantasy-like character. When they are compared to Bach's beautifully integrated, consistent, and exquisitely colored suite movements, they must be considered as relatively inferior works. This is not to belittle Handel to the point of denigration. Isolated movements in the suites have great beauty, imagination, and originality. It is their integration into a well-formed whole which suffers.

THE GREATNESS OF J. S. BACH

We have saved the best for the last. The world did not resound to the genius of Johann Sebastian Bach (1685-1750) in his lifetime or for some years after, but the nineteenth century saw a steady growth in his recognition as possibly one of the two greatest musical geniuses of all time. (The other is Mozart.) Keyboard players are especially indebted to him. His splendid production of suites, six "French," six "English," six Partitas, would in themselves have sufficed to set him on the loftiest pinnacle of baroque keyboard composition. When we add to them the toccatas, the 15 two-part and 15 three-part Inventions, the Chromatic Fantasy and Fugue, the Italian Concerto, and the Little Preludes and Fugues, we may consider that he has more than fulfilled his keyboard obligation to his genius. But then we must hear with awe and delight his amazing 48 Preludes and Fugues comprising the Well-Tempered Clavier and feel that we have been blessed beyond our fondest expectations. To cap the climax, there is the set of perhaps the greatest variations ever written called the *Goldberg* variations after the harpsichordist whose aristocratic employer, Count Kayserling, commissioned them and paid a princely sum, 100 Louis d'Or and a golden goblet, for the piece.

Bach's work bears the stamp of inevitability, the greatest single attribute of a composer, which means that each measure as it occurs sounds as if no alternate musical thought could have been conceived. Yet we know that he indulged in varied versions so that we wonder at the great conviction invariably received by the auditor. If the greatness of a work is measured by the balance between overall form and the mass of detail which inhabits that form, then Bach is indeed preeminent in the art. His technique of writing is impeccable, his variety of mood inexhaustible, his feeling for the shape and duration of each piece is as perfect, aside from a few of the earliest works, as it is possible to conceive. It is not surprising that Mozart was startled to hear a few of the fugues and view the parts to one of the great choral compositions with awe. He promptly arranged some of the fugues for string trio.

With Bach and Handel, the great Baroque era came to an end, and the overlapping of a new concept less intellectual, less ordered, simpler, far more personal and mannered began to obscure these giants of an enduring art. To look upon the Baroque with nostalgia would be a mistake since we should not want to remain inert in one era any more than we should want the world to stand still in space.

THE BACH FAMILY:
WILHELM FRIEDEMANN, C.P.E., JOHANN CHRISTIAN

With the end of the Baroque, a peculiar phenomenon took place in Europe. In France and England interest in writing for the keyboard well-nigh vanished and for almost a century, the instrument suffered neglect. The few pieces which were written were by obscure and little talented composers. Their compositions are to be found only in the historical collections housed in music libraries for the purpose of verifying their small historical impact. In Italy, a brave and sustained effort was maintained by a group of eighteenth-century composers who looked to the new genre in keyboard writing as an outlet for at least a part of their art. But this effort could not be sustained and by the nineteenth century, the keyboard in Italy was as defunct as in England and France.

Germany presented a totally different picture. The Bach family alone revealed a succession of fine composers who, though reverencing their great father, nonetheless went their own ways in pacing the keyboard art along new and exciting paths. Three of the sons were composers; two of them noteworthy. Wilhelm Friedemann Bach (1710-1784) was the eldest son. He wrote well if not in a distinguished style and cannot be considered important. The second son was Carl Philip Emmanuel Bach (1714-1788). His contribution to the development of keyboard composition was enormous. At least three of Germany's greatest composers freely acknowledged their debt to him. These three were Haydn, Mozart, and Beethoven. A great deal has been said about C. P. E. Bach. His worth as a composer of very beautiful music has never been clearly defined. Whether it is that he had the misfortune to be his father's son and the world cannot bear to conceive of two Bachs; whether it is that he has suffered the fate of the innovator who must have his inventions expanded and developed by his musical descendants; we find, as a result of the foregoing, a confusion as to his intrinsic and ultimate worth.

He wrote preclassic sonatas for the clavichord, many sets of six or more at a publishing. They are in the new style; that is to say, they are rarely contrapuntal, they are oriented toward harmony chiefly, with brief varied phrases, tuneful, charming, gallant, very emotional in the slow movements, expressing a degree of pathos bordering on the bathetic; they are above all prototypes of idiomatic keyboard writing. They fit on the keyboard and serve to promote the keyboard's potential; they exploit it and reveal its possibilities.

He was the father of the classic sonata. He took that element of the Italian overture represented by the sequence fast, slow, fast for the three movements. He took the French rococo simplicity and homophony, and to it he added his own German type of emotionalism, or Empfindsamkeit, to create by this synthesis something the musical world wanted and needed to depict a new age. In the sonata's opening movement he experimented with a new shape as evidenced by two key areas with one or two themes, a following section ultimately termed the "development," a recall or "recapitulation" of the first or "exposition" section and a close or "coda." He was varyingly successful, but it remained for the first of the great classic composers, Haydn, to set the form once and for all. Quite apart from this, he was writing very attractive and even beautiful music. His slow movements point the way to the nineteenth century and Romanticism because of their revelation of how subjective or personally revealing music can be. In his final movements, he turned at times to the French and wrote a Rondo or went back to the German suite and wrote a kind of gigue, sometimes greatly slowed and made lyric instead of rapidly staccato with the traditional triplet rhythm. His early sonatas, the "Prussian," are brilliant, gay, and sonorously rich in the slow movements. In the subsequent Württemberg Sonatas, published two years later, he wrote with greater deliberation and serious intent, though one wonders whether he did not lose something in the process.

Mozart's beautiful keyboard fantasias can be traced directly to those of C. P. E. Bach; his, in turn, can be seen in his great father's Fantasia from the Chromatic Fantasia and Fugue. The C. P. E. Bach fantasias are in such a fine vein that they may be termed written down improvisations. They begin with a quiet theme which gradually assumes the quality of a cadenza without bar lines and waywardly changing speed, texture, and content until one is aware that a fertile imagination and a fine keyboard technique are employed in a kind of wandering through the instrument's byways until the piece comes to an ordered close.

C. P. E. Bach's fame rests partly on his great pedagogical treatise, "An Essay On The True Art of Performing On a Keyboard." This extensive essay is not only valid in its prescription for finger technique but also illuminates many usages in the performance of the music of the period, such as correct tempo, understanding of ornaments, accompanying other instruments and improvisation. His treatise, together with that of Quantz's similar essay in respect to flute playing, give us the greatest overview of performance practice from the latter third of the seventeenth century to the middle of the eighteenth century.

Johann Christian Bach (1735-1782), the youngest son of J. S. Bach, likewise studied with his great father. Barely 15 years old at his father's death, he continued his schooling with C. P. E. Bach, who was then in his late thirties. Subsequently, he studied in Italy with a famous teacher, Padre Martini. He changed his religion, absorbed the Italian love of melody, and moved to London where he achieved considerable fame as a composer and wrote many keyboard sonatas. For two excellent reasons, he deserves attention. Many of his sonatas go all the distance in establishing the completely classic formula as exemplified in Mozart and Beethoven, not only in the three-movement framework but particularly within the first movement. The second reason for his claim to fame is the importance of his influence on the child, Mozart, who took three of his sonatas and expanded them into his first three concerti, with a solo piano part, an orchestral accompaniment and cadenzas. His impression was great enough to evoke Mozart's reverence, no mean achievement when we read of Mozart's attitude toward most of his contemporaries.

However, if we evaluate J. C. Bach's keyboard works without regard to any contemporary opinion, we are forced to find them lacking in spontaneity and imagination. They do not sparkle like the gallant works of C. P. E. Bach, nor do they exhibit either the variety of technical device or the poignancy of emotion of his older brother. They are not sufficiently virtuosic to arouse admiration. They are pedestrian rhythmically and are rather well suited as teaching examples in the early classic style.

Another reason for noting these works is the fact that several of his sonatas were clearly destined for the piano, still a primitive instrument but gradually improving and coming into growing favor.

The thrust, in Germany, of keyboard composition in the eighteenth century is still enduring in the twentieth century. Until the piano ceases to attract in public performance and in the home, it will probably receive the attention which began with the compositions of C. P. E. Bach.

SUGGESTED READING

Bach, C.P.E. *Essay on the True Art of Playing Keyboard Instruments*, (translated by W. Mitchell). New York: W. W. Norton & Company, Inc., 1949, pp. 1-22 (Introduction).

Bukofzer, M. *Music in the Baroque Era*. New York: W. W. Norton & Company Inc., 1947, pp. 108-111 (Froberger); p. 263 (Kuhnau); pp. 341, 342 (Handel); pp. 285-288 (J. S. Bach).

Bodkey, E. *The Interpretation of Bach's Keyboard Works*. Cambridge, Mass.: Harvard University Press, 1960. pp. 1-30 (Introduction and historical review).

David, H. T. and Mendel, A. *The Bach Reader*. New York: W. W. Norton & Company, Inc., 1945, pp. 306-312 (Forkel on Bach).

Geiringer, K. *The Bach Family*. New York: Oxford University Press, 1954, pp. 259-278 (J. S. Bach's keyboard works); pp. 354-360 (C.P.E. Bach's keyboard works).

Gillespie, J. *Five Centuries of Keyboard Music*. Belmont, Calif.: Wadsworth Publishing Co., Inc., 1965, pp. 119, 120 (Froberger); pp. 126, 127 (Kuhnan); pp. 127, 128 (G. Muffat); pp. 130-142 (Bach and Handel).

Kirby, F. E. *A Short History of Keyboard Music*. New York: The Free Press, 1966, pp. 98-101 (Froberger and Kuhnau); pp. 127-140 (J. S. Bach); p. 183 (J. C. Bach).

Landowska, W. *Landowska on Music.* New York: Stein & Day, Publishers, 1964. pp. 165-223 (Bach's keyboard works); pp. 236-243 (Handel's music).
Reeser, E. *The Sons of Bach.* Stockholm: The Continental Book Co., 1946. pp. 36-40 (C.P.E. Bach); pp. 60-62 (J. C. Bach).

SUGGESTED WRITTEN ASSIGNMENTS

1. What is meant by internationalism in music?
2. What would a fusion of styles bring to music as a good thing, and what might be a disadvantage?
3. In what respects did Froberger alter the toccata and the suite?
4. Why were the Biblical Sonatas of Kuhnau popular?
5. Why must we consider Handel's suites inferior to Bach's?
6. Name four types of composition composed by J. S. Bach.
7. What two composers marked the end of the Baroque period?
8. What are characteristics of the preclassic sonata as embodied in the gallant style?
9. Why is C.P.E. Bach termed the father of the classic sonata?
10. Besides the sonata form, what does Mozart owe to C.P.E. Bach?
11. What subjects are contained in C.P.E. Bach's treatise?

SUGGESTED LISTENING

1. FROBERGER—Suite No. 14, G Minor (on the clavichord)
2. KUHNAU—Biblical Sonatas
3. TELEMANN—Fantasias
4. J. S. BACH—*Chromatic Fantasia and Fugue; Capriccio on the Departure of a Beloved Brother; Partita No. 2, C Minor*
5. C. P. E. BACH—Sonata in A (Prussian)

SUGGESTED ADDITIONAL LISTENING

1. J. C. BACH—Sonatas
2. FROBERGER—*Tombeau de M. Blanchroche;* (clavichord) Fantasia, Ricercar
3. HANDEL—Suites
4. BÖHM—Suites
5. BUXTEHUDE—Capricciosa
6. FISCHER—*Passacaglia* and *Passepied*
7. KRIEGER—Suites
8. W. F. BACH—Fantasias and Fugues
9. J. S. BACH—Toccatas

6

The Classic Composers (1750-1827)

THE GROWING IMPORTANCE OF THE PIANO

At this time in history, the piano began to emerge, despite its evident shortcomings, as the desirable and preferred keyboard instrument over all others. Even the organ, so massively installed in church ritual,

Figure 9. Two-manual (keyboard) Harpsichord, believed to be the property of Joseph Haydn, in the Art History Museum, Vienna. (From F. J. Hirt's **Meisterwerke des Klavierbaus,** p. 28, 1955.)

suffered a decline in compositional interest and only returned to favor in the middle of the nineteenth century. The later classic composers of Germany appreciated the pianoforte and gave impetus to its development by writing sonatas whose profundity, intensity, and, finally, whose demand for volume literally pushed the manufacturers into heroic efforts to develop the kind of instrument able to justify the speed, diversity, and ultimately the grandeur of the compositions written for it.

THE THREE GREAT GERMANS

A great triumvirate of Teutonic composers emerged, Joseph Haydn (1732-1809), Wolfgang Amadeus Mozart (1756-1791), and Ludwig Von Beethoven (1770-1827), within the scope of whose compositional production is contained all that pertains to the classic era and in whose work is readily evident the seed which would flower into Romanticism. All three were aware of and influenced by C. P.E. Bach. Not only were they impelled to experiment further along the structural lines which he struggled to frame into an enduring edifice, but the variety and quantity of his idiomatic devices for the keyboard gave them food for pianistic thought, and the advantages of the new instrument over the clavichord provided the stepping stones for two techniques of writing. One was in the direction of lyric or soulful melodies, which C. P. E. Bach used almost exclusively in his slow movements. The other was in the expansion of rapid and lengthy passage work, continued over many measures in the rapid movements. C. P. E. Bach would almost always break off after a short spurt. Then, the piano also allowed them, with its wide dynamic range, to write dramatically with plateaus of sound previously impossible, given the clavichord's meagre voice or even the harpsichord's greater volume.

However, it must also be realized that of Haydn's fifty-odd keyboard sonatas, only the last several were positively written with the clear intention of pianoforte performance rather than the harpsichord. (Most of Mozart's sonatas are for piano.) This is made evident through the setting forth, in the latest works, of dynamic and articulation directions such as legato and staccato. It was a convention to refrain almost completely from such indications in harpsichord music, leaving the phrasing and dynamic choices up to the performer.

THE SONATA FLEXIBILITY

It must be emphasized once again that the musical art is ever dynamic and never static in the minds of great composers. We say that

Johann Christian Bach and then Haydn and Mozart and Beethoven
set the classic sonata into its final and great mold and hardened it
there but we are not altogether right. While it is true that the bulk
of their sonatas conformed to the clear classic formula in the first
movement of two key areas, two themes, exposition, development, recapitulation, etc., the slow movement an ABA form, the last movement
a rondo, it is also true that they wrote many exceptional keyboard
sonatas which avoided this format. Haydn wrote variations in the first
movement of a sonata in G, he avoided a second theme in a C♯ minor
sonata and merely repeated his first theme in a transposed key; at
times he did not use the conventional key relationships of tonic and
dominant for his themes. He wrote a minuet for his final movement
frequently instead of the usual rondo and even wrote, along with
Mozart, a first movement form at times and set it in the final movement position. He was more experimental than his admired younger
friend, Mozart, and learned from him less than Mozart took from him.
Haydn was less lyric than Mozart and tended to write interjection-type
themes containing a greater variety of rhythmic devices than Mozart.
Mozart tended generally to write longer, smoother lines of melody,
very beautiful ones, but he paid a price for so doing, since the kind
Haydn wrote lent themselves, because of their variety, to ease of development. Haydn took such full advantage of this that there were
times when his inventive "delirium" led him into an imbalance, where
the development became the longest part of the first movement. Mozart's developments, as a result of his lyric lines of melody, are often
disappointingly short, and at times he even introduced new themes in
his developments. In their slow movements, Mozart's lyric genius showed
itself to its greatest advantage and here, as well as in the final movements, he proved Haydn's superior. His sense of continuity was superbly
manifest in his final movements; where Haydn constantly came to full
cadential stops, Mozart spun a web of interconnecting themes with
that beautiful sense of continuity and inevitability which is the evident
hallmark of greatness. Haydn wrote fifty-odd sonatas, Mozart but
seventeen, partly due to his shorter life, partly due to his wonderful
ability to improvise whole sonatas in performance so that he almost
disdained putting any on paper.

   It must be said that in both their sonata repertoires there is considerable unevenness of accomplishment; Haydn wrote only about six
sonatas (out of 50) which may be considered as first rank works,
though many others have considerable charm and outstanding single
movements. Mozart did better; at least ten or eleven of his sonatas
are excellent, surpassing Haydn's finest. Beethoven, following last and

profiting by his predecessors' path-breaking, excelled them in many ways. At least 27 of his 32 sonatas are quite marvelous, exhibiting a breath-taking variety of moods, themes, constructions, and devices. One can only wonder at the breadth of his genius. He was far more interested in the keyboard than either of the others and even though he suggested in his sonatas a hundred different orchestral effects, from plucked strings to massed French horns, the total pianistic result is overwhelming and beautifully suited to the instrument.

THE BEETHOVEN SONATAS

Since whole volumes have been written about the Beethoven sonatas, it would be folly to attempt a serious analysis within a few paragraphs. It will have to suffice us to speak briefly of the approximately three periods they encompass. The most classic (in the Haydn-Mozart sense) are represented by the first ten, though there are "throw-backs" in some of the later ones, notably the famous *Waldstein,* Opus 53. In the early set, Beethoven wrote with a chiseled and deliberate objectivity as evidenced in strictness of form, transparency of texture, rarity of wide register usage, and an emphasis on these qualities rather than emotional intensity. Beginning with the two sonatas of Opus 27, including the soulful *Moonlight* and even including the *Funeral March on the Death of a Hero* (a movement from Opus 26), he entered upon a greater emotional or romantic-tending period marked by formal experimentation, frequent tempo changes, lyrical long lines of melody, lower and wider register usage, thicker textures, and an intensification of emotional values. The so-called *Tempest* and *Appassionata* sonatas (titles bestowed by others, not Beethoven) and finally the exciting *Farewell* sonata (of which the first three melody tones represent the word in German) are examples of this trend away from a formal reserve and toward emotion.

Finally, the late sonatas from Opuses 101 to 111, comprising the last five sonatas, are works in which Beethoven achieved the highest plane of intellectual-emotional synthesis. Three of them have fugues for final movements. They enjoy a combination of form and freedom within that form which is appreciated with ever greater admiration on repeated hearing. The first movements of both Opuses 101 and 109 are startling in the tempo contrasts between first and second themes. The greatest sonata, as well as the longest, is the *Hammerklavier,* Opus 106, whose performance time is more than forty minutes. The first movement is surprisingly emotional considering the almost constant use of contrapuntal device in its development, and the slow movement

Figure 10. Grand Piano, gift of Thomas Broadwood of London to Beethoven, 1817, in the Hungarian Historical Museum, Budapest. (From F. J.
Hirt's **Meisterwerke des Klavierbaus,** p. 47, 1955.)

position, normally second in movement sequence, is replaced by a
scherzo with unexpected metric alterations. The slow (third) movement is so beautiful besides being so difficult to sustain that it has
been the despair of performers, and the great fugue with its intro-
ductory and puzzling fantasia presents a nightmare of difficulty in

performance and memorization. The sonatas end with the Opus 111, marked by its abbreviated length of two movements only, and the late penchant of the composer to write at the extremes of the keyboard, frequently omitting the usually much-used middle register and producing a unique effect, which might be termed austere. The variations comprising the slow movement are so transcendently beautiful, it is clear Beethoven felt no more music need follow this utterance, and he artistically refrained from attempting to depart from the esthetic goal achieved at its close.

THE CLASSIC FANTASIA

Mozart paid musical homage to C. P. E. Bach in still another way. He wrote four fantasias and modeled them very closely on the C. P. E. Bach prototypes. They are multisectioned pieces, beginning slowly, and either ending rapidly or returning after one or two interludes to the slow beginning. They have, as do their models, an improvisatory quality and are variously simple to difficult to perform.

THE VARIATIONS

Apart from three trifling variation sets and the variations in his sonatas, Haydn wrote but one set in F minor, with a theme so long and varied that he wrote only two variations and a finale. Though it is a lovely work, it is evident that he had not much interest in keyboard variations. Mozart showed greater interest but made it evident that, despite a large number of variation works, he was either unaware of the possibilities or did not desire to experiment largely with the variation concept. A few of his middle period variation compositions introduce cadenzas and exploit the virtuosic possibilities suggested by this written-out type of improvisation, but by and large, his variations have charm without greatness or remarkable outstanding qualities.

When we view Beethoven's variations, we find he groped carefully through early variation works until, with the famous Thirty-Two Variations in C Minor, he suddenly found himself the master of a concept of keyboard writing without limit in its potential, and forthwith wrote three of the greatest sets of variations the literature can reveal, the aforesaid Thirty-Two Variations in C Minor, the *Eroica* Variations, based on two themes from his great third symphony and, finally, the transcendent Diabelli Variations on a theme, trivial in itself, by the publisher-composer of that name. What Beethoven saw and seized was the transmutability of a theme, either rhythmically, harmonically, thematically, texturally, in tempo and register, to depict the infinite variety of emotions experienced by humanity. Not since the *Goldberg* Variations of Bach, which are monuments of beauty and device, but emotionally restricted with intention, was keyboard invention carried to greater heights. And with these last sets of variations, Beethoven set the style for the nineteenth century, when the composers Schumann and Brahms used them as a springboard for their essays in variation writing, carrying them to a bewildering conclusion wherein the original theme of their variations is often virtually impossible to trace in their musical metamorphoses.

Mozart and Haydn showed a strong Italian influence in their sonatas. They are sparkling in the rapid movements and usually thin in texture. The French influence in Mozart is easily discernible in his variations, modeled after the rococo type emanating from the late seventeenth century. His themes in successive variations are broken down into increasingly shorter valued notes, giving an impression of gathering momentum after the old French "double" pattern. Beethoven became so individualistic that though we can trace influences, they are overlaid with the force of his own creative intent and we are reluctant to point to any one movement and say it sounds Italianate, French, or Germanic.

THE ENSEMBLE WORKS; THE CONCERTI

In their ensemble music containing piano, the three again present interesting contrasts. Haydn's piano trios and piano concerti are so light as to deserve the appellation trivial. Mozart, on the other hand, wrote trios in which his wonderful lyric gift, abetted by his fertile invention, resulted in exquisite masterworks, while in his many concerti he added to his innate lyricism a consciously varied virtuosity, as unique as it is beautiful, since it represents a perfect wedding of display and tuneful song within the same passages. This explains why pianists agonize over their Mozart performances since this lyric virtuosity is extremely difficult to project. And if it is not successfully projected, the performer's failure is painfully evident.

Beethoven, as ever the one to profit from his mentor's models, has written a monumental trio repertoire, in which the possibilities inherent in the three instruments in ensemble are nearly exhausted. Trios like the "Archduke," called after the one to whom it was dedicated, or the "Ghost" trio, the slow movement presumably inspired by Macbeth, give an illusion in sound of more drama and emotional depth than one could conceive possible in three instruments alone. In his five concertos, he goes from a post-Mozart charm in the first to a majesty and robustness in the "Emperor," the fifth, which makes one wonder how one mind, even that of a genius, could encompass such a span of musical evolution, almost as if he had lived more than one lifetime. Though Mozart wrote more than twenty-five concertos, he does not span anything like the emotional or even technical gamut that Beethoven displayed in but five concertos. This is not to detract from Mozart's greatness but merely to observe that Beethoven was an innovator whose every experiment turned into a success and pointed the finger in another direction piano composition might take.

The latter eighteenth century has been called the age of reason, because it witnessed the development of and respect for the use of the intellect as distinct from the fervor of religious feeling. Emotion was considered truly acceptable only when it was restrained and channeled into a work of art with balance, symmetry, and clarity.

SUGGESTED READING

Badura-Skoda, E. and P. *Interpreting Mozart on the Keyboard.* New York: St. Martin's Press, 1962, pp. 1-26 (Introduction and general view of his music).

Burk, J. N. *The Life and Works of Beethoven.* New York: Modern Library, 1946, pp. 415-417 (first sonata); pp. 419, 420 (Pathétique); p. 431 (Waldstein); p. 432 (Appassionata; p. 438 (Les Adieux).

Ferguson, D. *The Piano Music of Six Great Composers.* New York: Prentice-Hall, 1947, pp. 21-38 (Beethoven).

Hutcheson, E. *The Literature of the Piano,* 2nd edition. New York: Alfred A. Knopf, Inc., 1949, pp. 80-113 (Beethoven Sonatas and smaller works).

Newman, W. S. *The Sonata in the Classic Era.* Chapel Hill: the University of North Carolina Press, 1963, pp. 454-461 and pp. 475-480 (Haydn and Mozart); pp. 501-507 (Beethoven).

Shedlock, J. S. *The Pianoforte Sonata.* London: Methuen and Co., 1895, pp. 111-130 (Haydn and Mozart); pp. 160-191 (Beethoven).

SUGGESTED WRITTEN ASSIGNMENTS

1. How did the classic composers encourage and even force the development of the piano?
2. What is the classic formula for a sonata first movement?
3. What were the differences between the sonatas of Mozart and those of Haydn in regard to motivic writing, lyricism, development section of the first movement and the continuity of the final movement?
4. Describe the structure of Mozart's Fantasies.
5. Compare Mozart's, Haydn's, and Beethoven's interests and accomplishments in variation writing.
6. How many periods are represented in Beethoven's sonatas and what are the differences or characteristics of each period.
7. What are the differences in the ensemble music of the three composers?

8. Why do the compositions of the classic composers sound superficially alike?

SUGGESTED LISTENING

1. HAYDN—Sonata in E♭, No. 52
2. HAYDN—Variations in F Minor
3. MOZART—Variations on *"Ah, vous dirai je Maman"*
4. MOZART—Sonata in C Major, K. 330
5. MOZART—Fantasia in C Minor, K. 475
6. BEETHOVEN—Sonata, Op. 2 No. 2
7. BEETHOVEN—Sonata, Op. 109
8. BEETHOVEN—32 Variations in C Minor

SUGGESTED ADDITIONAL LISTENING

1. HAYDN—Sonata No. 34, E Minor
2. HAYDN—Fantasy in D Major
3. HAYDN—Sonata No. 50 in C Major
4. MOZART—Variations on *Salve Tu, Domine*
5. MOZART—Fantasia in C Minor, K. 396
6. MOZART—Sonata in A Minor, K. 310
7. MOZART—Sonata in B flat Major, K. 333
8. BEETHOVEN—The Diabelli Variations
9. BEETHOVEN—Bagatelles, Op. 119 and Op. 126
10. BEETHOVEN—Sonata Op. 81A *"Les Adieux"*
11. BEETHOVEN—Concerto No. 4, G Major

Romanticism: Germany, Hungary (1800-1900)

It is always difficult to define terms in art since the definitions use words which are susceptible of varied meanings. No one has clearly defined a "phrase" in music, and terms like "motive," "consonance," or "dissonance" are only capable of approximate descriptions. Thus, apart from citing coordinates in time, "classicism" and "romanticism" may as well be defined by the words objectivism and subjectivism as by saying that form and intellect are characteristics of classicism while emotion and spontaneity are hallmarks of romanticism. The romantic view is dominated by a flaming desire to become an integral part of and even a central pivot of the universe; the arch-ego of the romantic conceives the universe as a hugely personal entity revolving about itself.

MUSICAL CHARACTERISTICS

Romanticism in music has some of the following lineaments: a harmonic enrichment through the subtle alterations of well-known chords, so that their progressions become increasingly varied and complicated; this complexity is intensified by the increased use of key changes or modulation, used in ways never before essayed. Melodies are spun out in long ascending and descending lines without rhythmic variety or the use of combinations of rhythmic motives, the latter so characteristic of classic and baroque music. The inevitable reappearance of the bar line after a consistently regular number of beats is disturbed; the bar line is displaced, so that the former order of a bar line every four beats (as an example) may be rudely interrupted by one bar of three beats or even five (an unheard of number in classic music). Polyrhythms are increasingly evident (groups of three notes played simultaneously against groups of four or five notes) as are other rhythmic devices. The shape of the music, so fascinatingly complex in classic music, simplifies itself into ternary form for the most part, since complex form infers an intellectual discipline at variance with the precepts of romanticism.

The intent of the above concatenation of devices harmonic, melodic, rhythmic, etc., is a kind of music which breathes intense individuality, like a personal credo. It is a music which, in the mind of the hearer, is susceptible of interpretation in the most easily understood, human terms. The music can be full of longing, melancholy, delirious happiness, tender love, nostalgia, boldness, boisterousness—in short, very human. When Beethoven's music is playful, it has a kind of Jovian mirth. There is an Olympian quality and an austerity about the classics, but there is a down-to-earthiness about the romantics. We listen to the classics with awe and admiration and feel uplifted by them, but we wallow in empathy with the romantics and become one with them and are not transported to Olympian reaches.

One more new characteristic permeates romantic piano music. This is virtuosity, "show-off" ism, which was briefly revealed in Mozart concertos and variations, by-passed Beethoven whose brilliant passages were always fraught with the deepest musical significance, and finally emerged as feats of pianistic derring-do in the music of the romantics.

THE COMPOSERS AND THEIR MUSIC

Carl Maria von Weber

The earliest romantic composer is Carl Maria von Weber (1786-1826). He was sixteen years Beethoven's junior but in his piano works he is truly a long generation later; he was a most brilliant pianist, with a pair of the largest "piano" hands in Europe. Then, he was irresistibly drawn into the new nationalism with its awakened love of Teutonic lore, and as a result, a growing antipathy toward foreign domination of German art. This is typically romantic, love of one's country above all others and, by inference, that country's art. His *Der Freischütz* is considered the first truly German opera. His piano works were written to show his ability; they abound in speedy and not very meaningful passages, great hand stretches, tremolos in operatic imitation portraying excitement or, subdued, portentousness, and long melodic lines which rise and fall like great sighs contrasted with whirlwind tempi. His four sonatas, rondos, variations, and miscellaneous pieces have fallen into disrepute, though one or two like the sonatas in A flat major or E minor, when well performed, possess charm and interest because of what they preview. His harmony is enriched in the new fashion mainly in his slow movements and frequency of key change pervades most of his music.

Franz Schubert

With Franz Schubert (1797-1828), the greatest composer of romantic song, we encounter a composer in conflict with himself and tradition. In his lieder, he had no qualms; they poured out spontaneously and unaffectedly and were true effusions. But he did not trust this view of pianism; he admired Beethoven, not for his great individuality alone, but for his mastery of form and contrapuntal ability. As a result of this dichotomy between his natural spontaneity and his longing for the intellectual discipline imposed by the sonata form, he fell between two stools, writing illustriously beautiful melodies which did not lend themselves to the necessitous dismemberment of themes in development sections and achieving, with his spontaneity, his peaks of emotion before those places in the sonata where the climaxes should have transpired. There is, therefore, much "dead wood" in his sonatas and one of the great weaknesses of romanticism is sadly revealed—that is, the inability successfully to develop and sustain musical ideas for extended composition. He proves it; his short compositions, the Impromptus, Musical Moments and Dances are imperishably lovely. Much has been made of his great Fantasy in C, called the Wanderer after the theme which is identical with a song of that name. It may be said that it is a great piano work in spite of its shortcomings. Its theme is short and without sufficient rhythmic variety. It is episodic, stopping and starting, changing mood and tempo radically. And yet the genius of Schubert still makes it beloved, harmonically, texturally and, above all, emotionally. He was not a facile pianist and many of the passages in his music lie awkwardly for the hands to play, so that it is a pianistic triumph to achieve the smooth legato required of his lyricism or to play the frequently simultaneous passages in both hands with accurate facility.

Felix Mendelssohn-Bartholdy

If Franz Schubert presents certain conflicting elements in his piano music, there are none in the music of Felix Mendelssohn-Bartholdy (1809-1847). A preeminent composer whose talent enjoyed every benefit in its development, he wrote, in his short 38 years of life, a very respectable amount of music, of which a considerable quantity was for keyboard performance. However, it must be added that his music has shortcomings of a kind never attributable to the genius of Schubert. These lacks have caused his music to decline in popularity to the point where only a small fraction is studied and only a minute amount publicly performed. His music for the piano, with certain exceptions, lacks depth and intensity. There is fruitless speculation as to the reasons for this; he was a child of good fortune, rich, doted upon, personally ingratiating and well-mannered. There was none of Beethoven's tragic rudeness, none of Schubert's sad financial plight to mar the unbroken serenity of his life, and some think this may have stunted his emotional development. But learning, facility, and intelligence he had in large measure.

In his *Songs Without Words,* short mood or character pieces for the piano, he exploited a quite new if not original style. As the title suggests, he wrote a quasi-vocal line in the soprano position of the instrument and simultaneously accompanied it with the left hand and the lower fingers of the right hand. This calls for unusual dexterity on the pianist's part for two different textures and volumes are to be heard at the same time. The pieces, therefore, are fine studies and their simple ABA form (for the most part) makes them easily comprehensible if difficult to execute with true melodic legato. There is a wide variety in these short works of which the above style is a frequent example. Some are very rapid, requiring a miscellany of touches and a virtuosity stamping them in the nineteenth-century mold. The lyric melodies are romantic exemplars, breathing a gentle nocturne-like longing, and the harmonies make generous use of the recent expansion in that area.

His least works are his sonatas, which are superficial, poorly sustained emotionally, trite and dull. His finest piano composition is his Serious Variations wherein his great power of invention coupled with his profound knowledge of the piano's resources results in a brilliant work capable of holding its own with those of his great contemporary, Schumann, and their great successor, Brahms. In these variations, Mendelssohn achieves the true nineteenth-century variation concept, one where only the most tenuous thread at times ties the variation to its thematic model. This latitude in invention results, in the work of these prominent composers, in a species of purely romantic composition wherein each variation outlines, in terse form, a complete mood, almost a complete piece of music, yet provides part of a whole, like a pattern in a mosaic.

Mendelssohn's knowledge was sufficiently comprehensive to make him adept in writing six Preludes and Fugues, works consummately fashioned in contrapuntal technique, yet inevitably breathing a romantic spirit. The preludes, like Bach's, are étude-like in their use of repeated pattern, but completely romantic in their melodic and harmonic progression. The fugues, while finely wrought contrapuntally, are still basic in their harmonic orientation, so that one is overwhelmingly aware of their harmonic background even more than of their imitative part writing. The best known is the E minor with its Baroque fugal devices. The F minor has a melting prelude melody with subtly changing harmonies in repeated chords and a brilliant staccato fugue which tends to deteriorate into a strong scherzo after the exposition without much polyphony.

Robert Schumann

With Robert Schumann (1810-1856) we arrive at full-blown romanticism, replete with strengths and flaws. His music is full of fire and tempestuousness; it is so spontaneous in effect that one realizes at once that it has been composed at top speed and with little revision. The beauty of his melodies, the variety of pianistic devices, the wealth of harmony, his intriguing and experimental rhythms are all offset by the cracks in his musical armor, the inability to develop, the episodic quality of his form, the emotional peaks reached in all too few measures with nothing left but to start over on another musical tangent. These faults brought him the calumny of his critical contemporaries who honored him more for his literary gifts than his compositional ones. He began his musical career late, owing to parental opposition, and after the self-inflicted accident which interrupted his piano career, he began serious composition with his *Abegg* Variations at the age of 20. With this title he initiated an extramusical habit. Meta Abegg was a young lady who interested him, and on the letters of whose name he constructed the theme of the variations. Usually following the completion of a piece or suite of pieces, he affixed titles which the music suggested to him. In these variations he presents a fine preview of the style to which he adhered with various expansions during the rest of his life. This set of variations, together with his great set entitled Symphonic Études (1834) shows him at his best, full of invention, lyricism, and spontaneity.

Apart from the Symphonic Études, the other large-scale works, while uneven in beauty and finish, nonetheless show a loftiness of purpose, an immense passion and largeness of concept at variance with his ability and love of composition of small character pieces. The great Fantasy, Op. 17, in C Major (1836) is a three movement work ending with the slow movement. The first, unevenly divided into fast and slow sections in a rough ABA form, has great drama and pathos in spite of its meandering lines, its petering-out tendencies and bursting renewals of energy. The second movement, a grand march relieved by a lyric-scherzando episode in the middle, uses arpeggiated chords, contrapuntal devices, and a measured rhythmic tread, to end in leaping contrary figures in both hands like fireworks exploding in a night sky. The last movement has such supernal beauty of lyricism that it might be the quintessence of all avowals of love.

His third great work is a suite entitled *Kreisleriana* after an E. T. A. Hoffmann character, a well-nigh mad music conductor whose eccentricities exemplified the romantic artistic tradition. The music is wondrously varied from its étude-like opening through lyric, dramatic. scherzando and fairy dance episodes to end in two low muted notes on the piano, a work which, in its fanciful exploration of the soul of humanity, achieves a tenderness, a quality of man-not-God which nonetheless is wholly complimentary to the human psyche.

Of his three sonatas, only two are worthy of more than cursory attention. The Sonata in F♯ minor illustrates his affinity with Schubert, beautiful melodies, clever rhythms which, when interwoven, fall short of their purpose and produce an overlong, formless, and episodic maze. The G minor sonata is better but still not a truly successful work; neither the first nor second themes of the first movement are susceptible of development; they fit together poorly and produce an artificiality in their juxtaposition. The slow movement is lovely, partly because it is less than two pages in length. The scherzo is dashing, the last movement again has an indeterminate effect since it never culminates properly and its subsidiary themes are too far removed in tempo, rhythm, and mood from the leaping perpetual motion of the main theme.

There are a great many short works, among them the Intermezzi, the Fantasy Pieces, Novelettes, Woodland Scenes, Scenes from Childhood, and Album for The Young. There are beautiful pieces among them all, such as the *Bird As Prophet* from Woodland Scenes, *Soaring* and *In The Night* from the Fantasy Pieces, the *Novelette* in F♯ minor and the *Intermezzi* in E and B minor. But there are also sets that are played, as in the *Kreisleriana*, as suites, the *Carnaval, Papillons, Davidsbundler Dances* and *The Musical Joke From Vienna*. All of these have extramusical significance, the Carnaval pieces have intriguing titles and are almost all superficially motivated by a four-note group in different combinations, the names of the notes spelling in German a town, Asch, the home of a female friend. The Papillons are dances, gay little butterflies with an occasional popular song tune. The David's League Dances have reference to Schumann's fantasy society wherein he resides as several different characters at one and the same time, upholding the latest and most progressive in art through the medium of imaginary conversations. The *Musical Joke* is a reminiscence of a Viennese sojourn and has, in its several rather lengthy pieces, a sly reference to the Marseillaise (the performance of which was forbidden in Vienna) with writing of a somewhat inferior character for him, with the exception of a beautiful and tempestuous Intermezzo.

Mention should also be made of a brilliant and early Toccata, in the new nineteenth-century style, a piece of perpetual motion writing like a set of difficult études connected without pause. Where the seventeenth and eighteenth-century Baroque Toccata displayed, in disparate sections, facets of the keyboard art, the nineteenth-century Toccata displayed facets of virtuosity only, in one continuous and arduous keyboard flight.

This does not complete the roster of Schumann's keyboard music but it has been enough to reveal his main effort, to reveal him also as a champion and exemplar of an art which had taken a very different path and had revealed in its course that music could be newly thought of as an outpouring of the spirit through a warm and tender humanity.

Frédéric Chopin

Born in the same year as Schumann was Frédéric Chopin (1810-1849). In his short span he created more piano masterpieces than any composer before or since and he was history's only composer to confine himself almost exclusively to the keyboard. That he evinced wisdom in so doing is evident from a view of his non-piano works which are slight and largely unsuccessful. He wrote felicitously in large and small forms; his short pieces are, in their way, as gem-like as were Scarlatti's sonatas; his large utterances have an unequalled majesty in the romantic era and can be compared with the greatest classic keyboard sonatas. He had an unparalleled lyric gift; unlike Schubert, this was purely pianistic and not vocal in its conception, so that his melodies sing far better on the piano than they could hope to in the voice and demand the highest degree of legato, dynamic and voicing control on the part of the performer. Harmonically, he exploited every chord known in his time and his altered chord usage as well as his genius for delayed resolution of dissonance into consonance made for a color palette of enormous dimensions. Texturally, he wrought a revolution in the concept of the piano's possibilities, unveiling in an overwhelming number of his works new conglomerations of sound which directly inspired the much later Debussy.

He required a large and selective technique and pointed the way to its development in his twenty-seven scintillating studies which are so beautiful that one forgets the prime purpose announced in their title.

Some of his earliest works are neglected only because they are less wonderful than the plethora of later works. Among them are a *Krakowiak* and Variations on Mozart's *La Ci Darem Le Mano*. His small forms are his Waltzes, Nocturnes, Mazurkas, and Preludes. His waltzes are of varying length and in them he brings an idea at once to fruition. Until this time, a waltz was generally a very short piece, vide Schubert Dances, Beethoven, and Mozart, but Chopin strung several together and bound them by a refrain device, a recurring musical episode, which is not a main theme but a subsidiary one. Thus, a kind of rondo effect is achieved which allows the composer latitude in contrast and even in tempo. It is believed that he may have been influenced by Weber's famous *Invitation to the Dance* which is a prototype for this kind of construction. If so, it was a wise decision.

His nocturnes do not exploit a new concept but improve on one conceived by his contemporary and fellow Parisian, John Field. An Irish composer of no little fame (in his day), Field had constructed a gentle flowing melody set above and against a murmuring and recurrent bass figure of broken chords in triplet or quadruplet rhythm. Chopin enriched the nocturne by giving it dramatic impetus in a sharply contrasted B section, returning to the soughing, murmuring beginning in a recall section before the close.

His mazurkas are so unique that few pianists feel they can do them justice in performance. From very slow to almost dervish-like speed, they are episodic, constructed somewhat like the waltzes, but employing a variety of bass figures besides the waltz type, rhythmically wayward with deliberate tempo distortions, frequently modal in the eastern European tradition and harmonically and melodically vivid and surprising.

His Preludes are truly in the style, being, as were Bach's, unconfined to any form, length, or rhythm. They range from a 12-bar piece to almost 100 bars. The slowest tempo, largo, is to be found as well as presto, the fastest. Many of the very small ones are gem-like, exquisite and momentary mood evocations. Among the largest is a very difficult one to perform in E♭ with constant contrary leaps in both hands while a tender and soaring melody must be maintained. The

B♭ minor is a breathtaking perpetual motion bravura piece set against a sharply rhythmic figure in the left hand, while the great d minor which ends the set has a tocsin-like quality with its booming, repeated bass figure and aggressive, thrusting theme. There is one in f♯ minor with beautifully rapid interior figuration. Many of the short preludes are of a difficulty hardly commensurate with their size, as the D major and g♯ minor.

These short works marked the first time the prelude was to stand alone with no suite or fugue to follow. The concept of their freedom and the organization into all the keys goes back to Bach and actually back to the original Intonazione of the sixteenth century; an idea like a leaf on the wind is captured and frozen in a perpetual mold of sound.

Next in size of his works are the Polonaises, true evocations, not so much of a national dance as of the spirit which the dance represented. They are somewhat uneven in quality as they are in size. Among the truly great ones are the f♯ minor, clangorous, brooding, martial, and tenderly mazurka-like in turn; the ever popular one in A♭ major with its reiterated left-hand octaves set against a trumpet call theme and its meandering lyric contrasting passages; the "military" (not so called by the composer) with massed brass effects; the remote and melancholy E♭ minor; the intensely lyric and changeable c♯ minor; the nocturne-like B♭ major; and some lesser and less interesting ones.

Then there are the four scherzos. The first, in b minor, is a youthful work written when he was about 21 years old, and composed along with the two concertos and the first 12 études. It establishes a new view on the function of the title. This is no light, capricious work, but retaining the traditionally rapid three beat bar, a demoniacal driving, tempestuous, virtuoso piece relieved, after two repetitions of its A and B sections, by a slow languid melody, only to return to the A and end with a precipitous falling and rising passage. The most popular and best known scherzo is the second in b-flat minor which has many facets, starting with mysterious triplets, bursting into massed chords, then settling into a long line of rising song against a rolling bass. The center section is also divided by three, a low cello-like theme, followed by a lilting melody and culminating in a rapid, figuration-type passage. The end, after a recapitulation, is thunderous. The third scherzo in c♯ minor is undoubtedly the finest of the four with a rapid octave theme in staccato quarter notes contrasted with a chorale section relieved by ornamental figuration. This is interwoven with small developmental and bridge-type passages and ends with the usual whirlwind. In the last scherzo in E major, he essayed a kind of sustained stillness and grace which somehow never attained his desired objective and it falls short of the effect it might have had, had he pruned it with greater care.

The études, briefly mentioned before, may be considered next. They run the gamut from traditional finger studies through thirds, sixths, octaves, and rhythmic combinations to reach study motives never before seen. Studies like the *Winter Wind,* the *Harp,* the *Black Key* (the right hand never touches the white) explore unused technical paths. What is most remarkable about them is their beauty; they play well only when they are played with as much regard to their musical goals as to their technical ones. Their practical value is immense; they truly hold the key to his vast piano repertoire, and their study is repaid, not only by themselves in performance but by all his other works as well.

His impromptus, three in number, are not outstanding. Like Schubert's, they are conventional in their ABA form and differ only in that two begin rapidly, one more sedately.

His four Ballades have been compared in their loftiness of concept with the great Beethoven Sonatas. They are an extension of the ABA into an approximate ABABA. This enlargement is not so much through use of new material or developmental processes as through simple transposition and refiguration of previously stated material. The greatest is the last in f minor, and the least is the third in A♭ major.

There remain his two largest works, the Sonatas in b flat and b minor. They adhere to the conventional form throughout all their movements, save for the slow movement following the second movement scherzo. (There is a disregarded early sonata, never played.) The b flat minor has as slow movement the famous funeral march, and its greatest unconventionality lies in its final movement where both hands, playing the same notes separated by an octave, perform whirling and muted perpetual motion, so eerie that it has received the popular title of *Wind Over the Grave,* following the funeral march. Despite its undeniable appeal, this sonata is surpassed by the last in b minor, a work which demands every iota of the pianist's ability and reveals in superabundance the multitudinous facets of Chopin's genius. It may well be considered his greatest achievement.

The above comprise the bulk of the repertoire of this greatest of piano composers. There are some isolated pieces, a beautiful Fantasy in f minor which sounds extemporaneous yet reveals the greatest care in its organization; the exquisite *Barcarolle,* which starts as a simple song and reaches, through progressive enlargements, grandiose proportions; a *Berceuse,* whose monotonously repeated bass of only two harmonies is relieved by exquisitely figured variations in the upper voice; a *Tarantelle* which is a virtuoso piece that is too simple harmonically for complete success; some slight *Ecossaises* or Scotch Dances; the slight but difficult *Fantasy Impromptu,* so rarely played well since it is essayed by untrained children, and smaller works. For piano and orchestra, the two concertos are always popular, though the orchestral parts are so unsuccessful as to be almost redundant, and the *Andante Spianato* which may be considered in the same category.

If we have dwelled unduly upon Chopin, we must remember that in any volume on the piano and its literature, his position is preeminent and it would be illogical to neglect any part of his great production.

Franz Liszt

Since the nineteenth century was preponderantely a German one for the piano, it is a pleasure to cite a Hungarian, Franz Liszt (1811-1886), whose large repertoire of piano pieces has sadly dwindled in mid-twentieth century popularity. In his over 400 piano works, he exploited the modern piano to its greatest capacity and showed every composer who succeeded him what might be conceivably executed on that instrument. Even the later impressionists like Ravel found the study of his piano devices rewarding and the Russian fin de siècle composers drew heavily upon his resources when they wrote thunderous études, sonatas, and character pieces. He began his life as a virtuoso pianist, the greatest of his day, and it was only in the last part of his life that he eschewed virtuosity in his compositions. Even in his long religious period, he succeeded in cloaking his fervor with an extraordinary technical volubility.

By the time he achieved maturity, the piano was almost at the prime of its development. It had a 7-octave span, cross-stringing, copper bound bass strings, double escapement, and a steel frame. This meant that the sound it made could fill a large hall and that no limit might be set to the speed with which it might be played save the capability of the performer. Liszt spent many years extending the boundaries of his own endurance and speed, and wrote ever more difficult music which only he could play.

It is not surprising to hear that he specialized in étude writing since this style of piece was the accepted vehicle for virtuosity. His *Transcendental Études* (the word has reference to their transcendent difficulty) make demands of speed, clarity, and strength heretofore never contemplated. All the familiar difficulties are present in an exaggerated form, scales, arpeggios, chords, double notes as 3rds, 6ths, octaves, leaps, repeated tones, trills, etc. Outstanding are perhaps three of the Études. The one entitled *Mazeppa* has for its inspiration a Victor Hugo poem of an eastern European legendary hero who survived a several days' ordeal tied to a wild horse. The frenzied ride is graphically depicted, while it is relieved in a contrasting section by a seraphic dream or hallucination which breathes serenity. This is achieved by a transformation of the driving initial theme from minor to major while the double note picturization of drumming hoof beats sound muted and far away. The attempt to create in sound what the poet created in words is typically romantic and Liszt wrote few pieces which did not bear this extramusical connotation.

Like any true romantic, he found his greatest success in his shorter duration works. When he wrote long compositions he deliberately avoided classic developmental devices and instead wrote in a new manner, cyclically. In this style of writing, a group of themes, often numbering as many as four in his larger works, were repeated as many as three or four times with extensions. The repetitions were in the form of unofficial variations with extensive bridges connecting them. Also, in a work of several movements, each movement might begin with the same theme, suitably metamorphosed through the use of various devices, once with broken chord accompaniment, again through change of key and mode, being stated perhaps in simple chordal form or with interweaving figuration. Recognition was easy but monotony was avoided.

Another of Liszt's great *Transcendental Études* is *Will of The Wisp*. A simple theme, almost trite, is set against well-nigh absurdly difficult double note passages, the effect of which, when successfully performed, is breathtaking because of the two extremes. After that there is an untitled étude in f minor which has a soaring and bounding melodiousness with all manner of rapidly alternating chords, intricate rhythms, and passage extensions flashing to the ends of the keyboard.

The other études in the set run a gamut from languorous legato tone studies (*Paysage, Evening Harmonies*) through clangorously majestic chords and octaves (*Éroica*) to veritable blizzards of notes (*Chasse-Neige*).

Equal to and allied with this étude set is a set of transcriptions. These are felicitous, since they transform some of the famous caprices of Paganini, the greatest nineteenth-century virtuoso violinist, into equally wonderful piano music. We must note that transcriptions of this sort were most popular during this century and the skill of a composer might be shown equally well in his ability to metamorphose works of other media. No one could surpass Liszt in this field and he not only tackled instrumental works such as Paganini's violin caprices with enthusiasm but symphonies by Beethoven, operas by Wagner, Verdi, Bellini, Meyerbeer, etc., and songs by Schubert, Chopin, and others, often turning them into enchanting piano pieces and somehow succeeding in conveying the original composer's intent even though it was not realized upon the instrument of the composer's choice. Only Bach was his equal when he metamorphosed works by Vivaldi and others.

It would not be too daring to say that in some of the Paganini étude transcriptions, Liszt achieves a more felicitous result than does Paganini. The three most popular are the *Campanella,* another in *a* minor whose theme intrigued Schumann, Brahms, and later Rachmaninoff, so that, like Liszt, they all wrote variations of some sort on it as a foundation, and the E major which most nearly in its arpeggiated figures, approximates the original.

In his voluminous output, besides innumerable and indeed other very well written études, stand three volumes of character pieces entitled *Years of Pilgrimage.* Two are subtitled, one Switzerland and the other Italy. The third is posthumous and bears no subtitle. As might be expected, the majority of pieces from the Swiss collection have reference to that country, the *Chapel of William Tell, By the Lake of Wallenstadt, Valley of Obermann, The Bells of Geneva,* etc. None of these may be termed great music, even if *Orage* (Storm) has sound and fury effects and the rippling water evocation from *On The Bank of a Stream* and the undulant waves of *Lake Wallenstadt* are artfully depicted, if somewhat naïvely. The Italian set makes much of painters and poets. *Sposalizio* is after a Raphael painting, *El Penseroso,* after Michelangelo, *Petrarch Sonnets* are paraphrased, *Dante* (viewed through a Victor Hugo poem) and even a setting of a text, though for piano alone, by Salvator Rosa. Of these, *Sposalizio* is only pretty, at least two of the *Petrarch Sonnets* have been quite popular with their gently moving melodies interspersed with cadenza-like interludes, and the one extensive work, the *Dante Sonata* (in one movement), a somber opening piece followed by a staccato double-note theme, has an ominous quality in its relentless speed, interrupted by slower and still somber sections. For no easily determined reason, it is not an effective work in performance, and has been so recognized and avoided, unlike its far more famous counterpart, Liszt's famous b minor Sonata.

In this, perhaps his most famous work, he uses four powerful themes. The sonata, like the *Dante,* is in one movement, and the themes are metamorphosed in a transcendent manner. He writes a fugue on one of the themes in one of the sections. The whole is fraught with the kind of exalted tension so desirable to the romantic composers. Great

octave passages, arpeggios, thunderous chordal sections—to our sophisticated mid-twentieth-century ears, all of it has an overblown effect
and it is only when we hear this piece played by a still living great
artist of the Victorian past, that we can appreciate it because only
one of these somewhat anachronistic masters is still capable of playing
it in the "grand" manner with the complete conviction of utterance
the piece requires for a successful performance. Where Chopin's large
works draw the line of true genius in rarely overstating, rarely over-
dramatizing, Liszt all too often becomes overblown, oversententious in
his utterances and lachrymose instead of meaningfully emotional. This
is why his études and certain of his picturesque representations of
scenes will endure after his most deeply felt efforts will have been
rejected. His *Fountains of the Villa d'Este,* his études, like *Ride Of The
Gnomes, A Sigh,* and *La Leggierezza* will always have a willing audience. His religious pieces like *St. Francis Walking On The Waves,
Poetic and Religious Harmonies,* and his *Consolations* have only a
few loyal adherents.

Perhaps the most popular and periodically revived of his works
are his Hungarian Rhapsodies, or at least some of them. There are
nineteen and all are based on Hungarian gypsy musical ideas. They are
episodic, usually beginning with a slow quasi-improvised section, highly
ornamental, almost without rhythmic definition. This may be followed
by a more defined but still slow or measured section, or the two sections may be reversed in the order of their appearance. Abruptly,
following these, a rapid virtuoso dance section brings the piece to a
close. The use of gypsy modes, the frequent cadenzas, the dulcimer-
like imitations, the whirlwind technical passages employing scales and
arpeggios, chords, register leaps, all combine to create a kind of rendition which can bring storms of applause even from our sophisticated
concert devotees today. He added one more Rhapsody, using the same
construction, but employing traditional Spanish materials and entitled it *Spanish Rhapsody.*

Any evaluation of Franz Liszt has to take into account the following
credits: first, he recognized and fully exploited the technical resources
of the instrument; second, he revealed pathways harmonically and
technically that very many composers, particularly of the Russian and
French schools, explored to advantage. Such composers as Rachmaninoff, Balakierev, and Liapounoff openly emulated him. Ravel was
fascinated by his innovations in technique and in his *Gaspard de la
Nuit* and his *Miroirs* was moved to conceive further ideas whereby
technical devices might serve to depict watery background and a
kind of macabre poltergeist quickness. These are but a few who have
grafted on the striking Liszt root.

On the debit side we must list, first, his penchant for saccharine sweetness and perfervid emotionalism; second, his quasi-dramatic effects bordering on vulgarity; third, the naïvete of his musical portraiture which today seems musically juvenile. He had moments of greatness but they were few and far between areas of bombast. It is doubtful if he will ever regain the level of esteem he enjoyed at the end of the nineteenth century and for about a quarter of the twentieth century. His historical impact is great and he should be substantially represented in the repertoire of all pianists with concert pretensions.

Johannes Brahms

In direct contrast to Liszt, and still a composer of fine idiomatic keyboard works is Johannes Brahms (1833-1897). The contrast is provided by the realization that Brahms never wrote as a virtuoso composer for display, a characteristic which Liszt never sought to escape. Even in his slow, lyric works, Liszt wrote scintillating cadenzas. Brahms wrote one cadenza only, in the final movement of his first piano concerto in d minor and it is more a dramatic elongation of a pedal point on the dominant (or fifth scale step) than an actual display of technical prowess. Brahms criticized himself with less mercy than anyone ever showed to him and ruthlessly rejected the kind of sentimentalism which Liszt willingly embraced.

Brahms was a very serious student of music who pored over renaissance and baroque music. He wanted to be a conscious evolutionist and wrote conscientiously scrupulous form in his three largest works, the piano sonatas. In two of them, the first and third, he succeeded in at least the outward lineaments. The first movements are cleanly divided thematically and develop according to the best classic tradition. His slow movements are either in traditional song form or variation; his scherzi are in the romantic tradition, that is, they are heavily dramatic rather than playful; his final movements are in the traditional rondo shape. In his last sonata, Opus 5, he adds a "looking back" short slow movement which uses the first slow movement theme metamorphosed from a lovely lyric spun out melody into a somber brooding version interrupted by a shuddering fateful drum-tapping rhythm. In two of the slow movements, he reveals a very romantic trait (as in Schumann) of extramusical or extrapiano inspiration. The theme of the slow movement of his first sonata is, presumably, a Minnelied, or troubadour's song, and the equivalent theme of the third sonata is prefaced by a love poem by Sternau.

In only one respect does Brahms innovate and that is in his penchant for cyclic writing in these large works. A cyclic approach is one in which the composer binds or unifies the various movements of large works by reiterating his basic thematic material in various guises. Thus the theme of the final movement of the first sonata is a speeded up version of the initial theme of the first movement with a reduction of the original rhythm into uninterrupted triplets. Mention has already been made of the close relationship thematically between the second and fourth movements of the third sonata. The second sonata goes all the way and uses the same thematic material in all its movements. It is clear that Brahms felt this helped to establish an overall unity, yet he was sufficiently flexible not to overdo it and used it as a device with his customary discrimination.

The other works which represent his major piano effort are his variation sets, not many in number (six) and not all of equal importance. Only two may be thought significant, though all are tasteful. These two come last in the series: The *Variations On A Theme by Handel,* and the *Studies* (as variations) *on a Theme by Paganini.* The Handel variations are based on a theme used by Handel for variations of his own and it is wonderful to hear how Brahms metamorphoses this concise, clear, and precise melody and its simple harmonic structure into a great glowing romantic piece. In true romantic variation style, he writes variations which bear only the most tenuous relationship to the original theme and one can only marvel at the imagination which was able to conjure up such altered versions of the original. The harmonic background deepens by degrees until all manner of coloration is exposed. Rapid chord scales, musette reiterations on pedal points, extreme register changes, lightning mood changes, and, finally, a gigantically culminating fugue mark this pianistic tour de force, and still, one never for an instant feels that the technical devices take precedence over the musical concept. The same can even be said for the Paganini Studies in two "books" of 14 variations each. The trenchant utterances in all but the slow variations, while of superlative difficulty technically, are nonetheless of extreme seriousness musically and there is never a "technique for the sake of technique" outlook. The theme is the same which attracted the attention of Schumann, Liszt, and (later) Rachmaninoff and Boris Blacher (for orchestra). The flashing double note studies in thirds and sixths and octaves (with glissandi or slides), the crossed and interweaving fingers, the trills, the double-voiced legato studies, the intricate rhythm patterns, make for true études richly repaying study by the aspiring performer. Just as Chopin's *Etudes* and Liszt's *Transcendental Studies* contain the keys to all the difficulties of these respective composers, the Brahms' Paganini Studies serve a like purpose, indeed far more than his Exercises which are

largely confined to very dull and not too rewarding studies in polyrhythms.

An interesting observation concerns Brahms' shorter works. With the
exception of a few ballads (four), a scherzo, and his short waltzes,
the bulk of his Intermezzos, Capriccios, and Rhapsodies were written
during his last 20 years. He evidently felt that he could best fulfill
himself in these short forms after his earlier large essays. And it is
true that in these works he composes so flawlessly in regard to complete expression of his musical thought that one can only agree with
his unstated thesis that a truly romantic composer expresses himself
best in brief. This may be because the romantic concept is so spontaneous that it comes out in a short burst of inspiration, even if a
slow burst as in an intermezzo. Brahms disciplined himself to "think"
about his music as well as to "feel," in contradistinction to Schumann
and even Chopin and Liszt. Still, he wrote most nearly perfect music
when he ceased the effort to develop (an intellectual process). He
was capable of it but was more at home when he avoided it. Thus
these short works, running the gamut from light to dark emotion, thin
to thick texture, rapid to slow tempo, and involving a range of moods
from the darkest drama (E flat minor Intermezzo) to the most ami-
able serenade (Op. 76, No. 3) serve to express the true romantic spirit
in a manner that could never be revealed in any other age. Beethoven's
Bagatelles also contain great variety, but it is a variety tempered by
an objective and critical reserve wholly avoided in these Brahms'
works. They are intimate and personal, never vulgarly emotional, but
moving and revealing of the finest human quality.

The three Rhapsodies are like the smaller character pieces save for
their lofty strain and slightly greater length. Two are grandiose (Op.
79, No. 1, and Op. 119); one in g minor is smaller, more introspective
though less successful for that reason. The form is the same for all
these short works, a simple ABA and, in the Rhapsodies the B section
is altered to give an ABACA. The B section is almost always in marked
contrast to the A, though there are a few Intermezzi in which the
contrasting section is a mere extension of the A and does not use
different accompanying figures. (Op. 76, No. 4, in B flat is an example.)

Brahms' use of titles is typical of his era. He began with classic
titles, sonatas, and variations. These described the form. But then he
departed from this form indication and used Intermezzo, Capriccio,
Ballade, Rhapsody, and even one Romanze. These titles are sufficiently
vague to give the performer (and the composer) great leeway in conceiving and presenting them. Generally the Rhapsodies are grander and

longer than the other short works, the Intermezzi are gentle or graceful but encompass a variety of tempi from very slow to a fast moderato (Op. 116, No. 1 in C). The Capriccios are harsher, more aggressive or at times playful (scherzando), but still encompass a variety of tempi, beginning at a faster tempo than the slow Intermezzi, and reaching to a fairly rapid tempo only. The fast Brahms never attempts to reach the speed of the fast Liszt or Chopin and in the only exception, the Paganini Studies, the notes of the passage work are never ornamental as they so often are with the other two composers.

Brahms set the central European taste for the end of the nineteenth century. Almost all the minor German composers emulated him, and like all imitators, they sounded like inferior Brahms. Even the budding American composers like MacDowell, who studied in Germany, put on the Brahms' cloak and had difficulty divesting themselves of it. In Germany only the Lisztians and the Wagnerians fought his influence. There was not much conflict with Wagner since Brahms wrote no opera, but the Liszt school succumbed in Germany and achieved its greatest influence in Russia and France. The Russians linked Liszt and Chopin, flavored them with Russian national song, and served up a successful synthesis. The French studied those parts of Liszt having to do with harmonic strangeness and to an extent his technical devices

Figure 11. Engraved design for a grand piano by Thomas Sheraton, famous furniture creator. (Courtesy of J. Broadwood and Sons, England.) From James, plate 62.)

for portraying nature sounds, and deftly incorporated these elements as well as his orchestration into the peculiar aura of impressionism.

One more area of Brahms' accomplishment should be noted. He wrote two concertos for the piano, both large-scale works, the second of which is considered perhaps the greatest work of its kind in existence. Again, he manifests his seriousness by avoiding display, and though both concerti contain monumental difficulties, they are works written without the usual effort to display virtuosity. They stem from Beethoven whose early concertos are still in the tradition of pianistic commentary on orchestral themes but in whose last three concerti the piano emerges on a lofty plane of serious writing equivalent with the orchestra. Brahms carries this still further and even when the piano does not utter the theme as in the slow movement of the second concerto, its obbligato is moving and infinitely dignified.

Max Reger

One composer must be mentioned briefly though he deserves far more space than we can spare here. He is Max Reger (1873-1916) who is the latest born of romantic composers and who was influenced almost wholly by Schumann, Brahms, and Bach (in that order). His entire and quite large repertoire of early works is made up of short compositions, character pieces in the style of Schumann and Brahms, very romantic with typical textural turgidity. He indulges in rapid and pivotal key changes, unequal phrase lengths and frequent improvisatory cadenzas. His titles are very imitative of Schumann and Brahms, *Childhood Scenes, Loose Leaves, Intermezzi,* etc. His late works are large, including two huge sets of piano variations, fourteen on a theme of Bach, and twenty-four on a theme of Telemann. Both sets culminate in fugues. They are so elaborately written that they fit with the preceding three greatest sets, Bach's *Goldberg,* Beethoven's *Diabelli,* and Brahms' *Variations on a Theme by Handel.* His other large later works are for two pianos, an *Introduction, Passacaglia* and *Fugue* and two more variation sets on themes of Beethoven and Mozart. The admixture of romantic textures and baroque contrapuntal elements gives his music a fervor and solidity wholly suited to the Germanic temperament and explains his popularity in central Europe.

With Reger, and with a sense of inadequacy at the brevity of the foregoing, and a sense of guilt because of necessary omissions, we bring the romantic compositional scene in the Teutonic area to a close. This part of the western world cradled and culminated romanticism in music. The love of folk traditions and songs, the unsophisticated awe before the grandeur of the universe, the sentimental love of country, of children, of pets, all combined to produce a fervency in music that makes this the natural repository of that large repertoire included in romanticism of the nineteenth century.

SUGGESTED READING

Abraham, G. *The Music of Schubert.* New York: W. W. Norton & Company, Inc., 1947, pp. 111-148 (Piano music by K. Dale).

Dale, K. *Nineteenth Century Piano Music.* London: Oxford University Press, 1954, pp. 148-180 (examples of romantic music with explanation).

Einstein, A. *Music in the Romantic Era.* New York: W. W. Norton & Company, Inc., 1947, pp. 198-225 (the piano in the Romantic period).

Einstein, A. *Schubert.* New York: Oxford University Press, 1951, pp. 77-85 (early sonatas); pp. 283-290 (last works).

Ferguson, D. *The Piano Music of Six Great Composers.* New York: Prentice-Hall, Inc., 1947, Chapters 7-11 (Romantic composers).

Geiringer, K. *Brahms, His Life and Work.* New York: Oxford University Press, 1947, pp. 205-221 (keyboard works).

Gillespie, J. *Five Centuries of Keyboard Music.* Belmont, Calif.: Wadsworth Publishing Co., 1965, pp. 196-247 (Romantic composers); pp. 257-264 (Brahms, Reger).

Hutcheson, E. *The Literature of the Piano.* New York: Alfred A. Knopf, Inc., 1949, pp. 129-132 (Weber); pp. 136-140 (Schubert); pp. 144-150 (Mendelssohn); pp. 158-181 (Schumann); Chapter 8 (Chopin); Chapter 7 (Liszt); pp. 225-237 (Brahms).

Kirby, F. E. *A Short History of Keyboard Music.* New York: The Free Press, 1966, pp. 301-320 (Liszt); pp. 321-340 (Brahms).

Niemann, W. *Brahms* (trans. by C. A. Phillips). New York: Grosset & Dunlap, Inc., 1946, pp. 213-250 (the piano works).

SUGGESTED WRITTEN ASSIGNMENTS

1. Give a brief description of romanticism and cite the differences between classic and romantic viewpoints.
2. How do these differences appear in music generally and in piano music in particular?
3. Why do the following titles in piano music belong only to the romantic period: étude, impromptu, intermezzo, mazurka, Romanze?
4. What flaw existed in romantic composers and which composer suffered most from it?
5. Why are Schubert's sonatas not as successful as Beethoven's?
6. Were romantic composers generally more successful in writing long or short works?
7. Name as many differences as you can between the piano works of Liszt and Brahms.

SUGGESTED LISTENING

1. WEBER—Sonata in E Minor
2. SCHUBERT—*Impromptus,* Op. 90
3. SCHUBERT—Sonata in A, Op. 120

4. MENDELSSOHN—Serious Variations
5. SCHUMANN—Symphonic Études
6. BRAHMS—Variations on a Theme by Handel
7. BRAHMS—Piano pieces, Op. 76
8. LISZT—*Transcendental Études, Mazeppa* and *Feux Follets*
9. CHOPIN—Études, Op. 10

SUGGESTED ADDITIONAL LISTENING

1. WEBER—*Invitation to the Dance*
2. SCHUBERT—Sonata (posthumous) B♭ Major
3. SCHUBERT—*Wanderer Fantasy*
4. SCHUBERT—*Moments Musicaux,* Op. 94
5. MENDELSSOHN—Songs Without Words
6. SCHUMANN—Fantasia, Op. 17
7. SCHUMANN—*Carnaval*
8. BRAHMS—Sonata, Op. 5, F Minor
9. BRAHMS—Scherzo, Op. 4, E♭ Minor
10. BRAHMS—Rhapsody in E♭, Op. 119
11. LISZT—Hungarian Rhapsodies, Nos. 2, 6, 12
12. LISZT—Paganini Étude *La Campanella*
13. LISZT—Petrarch Sonnet No. 104
14. CHOPIN—*Barcarolle*
15. CHOPIN—Scherzo, B-flat Minor, Op. 31
16. CHOPIN—Fantasy, Op. 49

8

Russia and Late Romanticism (1835-1950)

NATIONALISM: THE FIVE

Russian music, like Russian pianism, represents a powerful romantic movement. Like any true romantic product, it is made up of national elements, folk song, folk dance rhythms, folk scales, and esthetically provides a grand emotional outpouring. Russia came late into the compositional field, being content at first to import Italian, Bohemian, and German composers. The most famous nineteenth-century Russian composers, the so-called Five, wrote hardly any keyboard music, writing instead operas, songs, and symphonic works. Two of these composers merit attention, Balakirev and Mussorgsky.

But before turning to their music, it would be well to discuss Russian keyboard music in general. The two greatest and coequal keyboard influences in Russian music stem from Chopin and Liszt and to this day the effect of these two composers can easily be discerned in the totality of Russian piano works. Even the Russian virtuosi are products of a training calculated to play this kind of music, lyrically fervent and brilliantly technical. In turn, they affect the type of composition practiced in their native land and thus the composer and performer act together to preserve a tradition largely discarded elsewhere in the western world.

The national element in their music was given great strength through an Imperial Commission of the Geographical Society to collect and publish Russian folk songs in 1897. Since the empire stretches from the Baltic to the Pacific, and from the Arctic to the Black Sea, the treasury of folk song, dance, and legend is undoubtedly the largest in the world; the variety and regionalism can easily be imagined.

THE COMPOSERS

Mili Balakirev

Mili Balakirev (1835-1910) is remembered for two reasons, his usage of native tunes and his brilliant exploitation of the Lisztian technique. His Sonata in B flat minor is not a work to last or even be attempted by present-day pianists who can find more musical reward with less effort in other Russian composers. His fame, however, rests on an Oriental Fantasy called *Islamey*, constructed on two themes (fast and slow) from the Caucasus area of Armenia. In this great technical tour de force, he uses the purest Lisztian devices of rapid double notes, octaves, furiously flying chords, and beneath it a great wealth of colorful harmony. These elements rescue what is essentially a fast, rather uninterestingly repetitive ABA with a still faster coda or ending section.

Modest Mussorgsky

The other pianist-composer of the Five was Modest Mussorgsky (1839-1881). Like most Russian composers of his day, he was a gifted amateur, in the sense that he earned his living through sources other than music. He has been immortalized in the piano libraries by a large suite of pieces which, like the Robert Schumann sets, have an extramusical motive to give them a semblance of musical logic. The work, *Pictures From An Exhibition*, has as its inspiration an exhibition of paintings and drawings by the artist Hartmann. The composer promenades via a repeated passage from one painting to another, pauses, and we hear the musical representation of the painting being viewed. The promenade interlude is imaginatively varied and the paintings, some somber, some fantastic, some crowded with activity, are masterfully portrayed.

Peter Ilich Tchaikovsky

Though Peter Ilich Tchaikovsky (1840-1893) enjoys just fame as one of Russia's greatest composers, his piano music is not comparable to his other works. Aside from two oversized and bombastic sonatas, he wrote salon music of inferior quality. His little *Troika* and his set of pieces called *The Seasons*, one for each month of the year, have some superficial charm. Everyone, however, knows of his famous Concerto in B flat minor, where, belatedly accepting the piano score corrections suggested by Nicholas Rubinstein, he succeeded in creating a masterpiece of romanticism to rival his symphonies.

88 russia and late romanticism (1835-1950)

Sergei Liapounoff
Sergei Liapounoff (1859-1924), as a member of the Commission, profited by the great folk music collection to write using thematic material from various byways of the Russian Empire. His large étude, *Lesghingka,* uses melodies and rhythms of the Lesghian tribe of southern Russia. This étude is one of twelve and is the only one still to be heard. His technique stems from Franz Liszt.

As we progress into the twentieth century, Russian piano composers become more prominent. This is not to say they become "modern" in sound but rather work to preserve the nineteenth-century flavor with its brilliant non-German figuration and its seductive harmonic alterations of basic chords. Three composers exemplify this tenacity of adherence to a former era. Though they are very akin in their approach to keyboard music, a wayward fate has placed one of them far ahead in popularity. The three composers are Alexander Scriabin (1872-1915), Sergei Rachmaninoff (1873-1943), and Nicholas Medtner (1880-1951). It is Rachmaninoff who has been selected as fortune's favorite.

Alexander Scriabin
Alexander Scriabin was the most daring of the three and the most romantic or individualistic in outlook. He began in the Russian tradition by writing Chopinesque short works, preludes, and études. They are good pieces, far more arresting and strong than those of his predecessors. But his originality, his urge to develop and expand led him to large works, ten sonatas and several "poems." In the sonatas, he began conventionally enough to write in the Liszt-Chopin tradition, but with his fifth essay in this form other elements entered. It is difficult to assess the worth of these new ideas as they betray his growing tendency toward mysticism and "ecstacy." These qualities, for which he began to construct chords based on the interval of a fourth instead of a third, allied with extraordinary difficulties in rhythm and technical devices, caused his reputation to diminish. Today, few pianists will essay his sonatas, particularly the late ones, feeling that they are not sufficiently rewarding for the effort needed to learn them. Certainly many of his compositions have power—almost too much power. This surfeit of feeling is presently shunned as a manifestation of poor taste.

Sergei Rachmaninoff
Sergei Rachmaninoff is beloved because of two concerti (out of four), the second and third. These solo-piano-with-orchestra pieces have

qualities of simplicity, immediate appeal lyrically, highly exciting virtuosity, and strong folk elements, a combination which, if tastefully executed, is a guarantor of success with the public. A third piece of this type, the *Rhapsodie on a Theme by Paganini,* holds almost equal rank in the public's estimation. Scriabin turned his back on the Five and went his own way toward Chopin, Liszt, and finally himself, without looking back. Rachmaninoff willingly embraced his national heritage, while doffing his hat quite as willingly to Chopin and Liszt. He wrote preludes, almost the worst of which have, exasperatingly, the greatest popularity, and *Tableau Études* which presumably are evocative of undivulged scenes and stories in the composer's mind. There are also two sonatas, two sets of variations, and various short pieces. His lyric gift, his folk references, his virtuosity in figuration, make for attractive, if thoroughly conventional writing.

Nicholas Medtner

Nicholas Medtner is the least appreciated of the three. As thoroughly traditional as Rachmaninoff, he is just as musical and quite as accomplished. Yet his romantic sonatas, his concerti, his *Fairy Tales* (character pieces) lie unplayed. Many of the short works are minor masterpieces, brilliant and effective for the keyboard, full of fine technical, rhythmic, and harmonic devices.

Serge Prokofieff

Undoubtedly the greatest Russian composer for the piano and thus far the greatest piano-composer of the twentieth century is Serge Prokofieff (1891-1953). Almost from the start of his career, he refused to follow the (by now) traditional piano path of Chopin-Liszt. His first sonata (of nine) is, to be sure, a purely romantic and traditional one-movement work. (He destroyed the other two movements.) It is still enjoyable, if naïve, and haltingly revealing the ignorance of youth. He was sixteen when he wrote it and revised it at eighteen. From his second sonata on, however, he demonstrates a rare combination of originality and an intransigent insistence on seeking his own harmonic, rhythmic, and textural path. The results are felicitous. All the sonatas are beautifully varied. They contain fine lyric elements, strong propulsive rhythm, textures varying from leanness to rich exotic chords, folk references metamorphosed into gay or demonic melodies, and sharply satiric utterances, terse and biting. Besides these monumental works, he has written a set of *Sarcasms,* short pieces employing polytonal (two or more keys simultaneously) elements, harsh harmonic textures, propulsive rhythm structures and surprising bits of lyricism. His *Fugitive Visions* are a group of extremely short pieces fulfilling their title. Some are impressionistic, others are visionary, still others are bursts of splenetic harshness. All are improvisational little masterpieces. His pieces for children are enchanting. His toccata is made like a mathematical equation and is a most exciting motor tour de force. His early Diabolical Suggestion is a melodramatic announcement of what he was already capable at 18 years of age.

Igor Stravinsky

Mention must be made of Igor Stravinsky (born 1882) not because of his piano accomplishment, since it is negligible, but because he is too great to be ignored. Though he was a fine concert pianist, he chose to deny the keyboard the fruits of his genius, writing only a few works and couching them in a somewhat unrewarding style, the neobaroque. His finest piece is a Concerto for two Solo Pianos (without orchestra). Though it is also in the above stated style, the four hands make a thick texture and the sounds of the interwoven themes and counterpoints disclose a variety and intricacy which is very delightful. The same cannot be said of his Sonata for one Piano, which is dry, perpetually repetitive in rhythm and sparsely written to the point where change in color quality is lacking. His Serenade in A is a bit more varied but not enough so as to render it highly attractive. There are four early studies in romantic style, not outstanding. Finally, there is also his unbelievably difficult transcription of three episodes from his ballet *Petrouchka*. He writes for keyboard with the kind of perfection of technique accorded to all his works; it is only that his desired effect does not coincide with that of most musicians and the music-loving public.

Dmitri Shostakovich

Dmitri Shostakovich (born 1906) is the most prominent of the Russian composers whose early experiments were tolerated to a point, when he received a nonappeal order to refrain and return to the traditional path. In his piano music, he has decidedly done so, only permitting himself puckish harmonies at times. His talent is great, however, and no imposed framework could be so constricting as to stifle it. He has written Preludes, completely aware that they are closely modeled after Chopin's. However, the folk element and a somewhat dry quality causes them to be quite different from their models, as also does the more dissonant harmony and the deliberate ballet-like humor. His 24

Preludes and Fugues are neobaroque, modeled this time on Bach. They are not as satisfactory as one might hope for in the light of his genius and fully developed technique of composition. They tend toward internal monotony of rhythm and harmony despite his scholarly use of all the known baroque devices. Certain exceptions occur, as in the one in D♭ major, when he introduces folk dance quality and a high degree of chromaticism (half-step progression) in the fugue. His two sonatas are not successful; the first has powerful qualities but owes so much to the first Prokofieff Sonata that it suffers from the imitation as well as overlength. The second is a modest effort without distinction but is nonetheless more purely Shastakovich than the first. His early three Fantastic Dances are light stuff but very charming. His two piano concertos are undistinguished, with the first considerably the better of the two since it has elements of humor and lyricism, much like ballet music.

Dmitri Kabalevsky

His contemporary, Dmitri Kabalevsky (born 1904), is more consciously nationalistic than Shostakovich and his piano music is somewhat more voluminous, with several sonatas, equally as many preludes and concerti, and a large and glowing body of children's pieces comprising all forms and styles in miniature, from variations through études, preludes, fugues, and character pieces. He fills a great need in contemporary study of the piano by very young children. These pieces are uniformly charming, vital, lyric, mood pictures that are a joy to study. The folk element is deliberately very marked in them and adds to their appeal.

Aram Khachatourian

The only other Russian composer who has attained prominence apart from his country is Aram Khachatourian (born 1903). His fame, however, is non-pianistic and he therefore should only be mentioned. He has written a Toccata which is studied and performed, unhappily, more than it deserves to be. It is a somewhat graceless mixture of nineteenth century and baroque elements, sadly trite and shallow. His piano concerto is a very showy affair, with brilliant parallel passages in both hands, a degree of dissonance, and employing Armenian folk elements in harmony and quasi-improvisation. It is not an enduring piece, but effective on first hearing.

Suggested Reading

Bertensson, S. and Leyda J. *Sergei Rachmaninoff.* New York: the N. Y. U. Press, 1956, pp. 200-202, and pp. 173-174 (Tableaux Études); p. 296 (Prelude).

Calvocoressi, N. D. and Abraham, G. *Masters of Russian Music.* New York: Alfred A. Knopf, Inc., 1936, pp. 450-498 (Scriabin); pp. 436-438 (Liapounoff); pp. 97-146 (Balakirev).

Collaer, P. *A History of Modern Music,* (trans. by S. Abeles). New York: Grosset & Dunlap, Inc., 1961, pp. 284-307 (Soviet music, Prokofieff, Shostakovich).

Gillespie, J. *Five Centuries of Keyboard Music.* Belmont, Calif.: Wadsworth Publishing Co., Inc., 1965, Chapter 21 (The Slavic Countries).

Hansen, P. S. *An Introduction to 20th Century Music.* Boston: Allyn & Bacon, Inc., 1961, Chapter 14 (Soviet Russia).

Kirby, F. E. *A Short History of Keyboard Music.* New York: The Free Press, 1966. pp. 363-370 (Russian music).

Leonard, R. A. *A History of Russian Music.* New York: The Macmillan Co., 1957, pp. 211-226 (Scriabin); pp. 227-250 (Rachmaninoff); pp. 295-321 (Prokofieff); pp. 322-340 (Shostakovich).

Montague-Nathan, M. *Contemporary Russian Composers.* London: Palmer and Hayward, 1917, pp. 54-69 (Scriabin); pp. 166, 167 (Rachmaninoff); pp. 238-251 (Medtner).

Nestyev, I. V. *Prokofieff.* Stanford: Stanford University Press, 1960, pp. 454-488 (Stylistic features).

Suggested Written Assignments

1. Name the two non-Russian composers who serve as pianistic inspiration for most Russian composers.
2. How were the Russian composers made aware of their wealthy national music heritage?
3. Did the "Five" contribute materially to Russia's piano repertoire? Why?
4. What three composers in Russia competed for fame during the first third of the twentieth century, and which one emerged as the public's favorite in piano composition?
5. What piano composer bids fair to become the most outstanding of this century?
6. What direction has the present Russian government encouraged composition to take?
7. Why is the future of Russian composition a matter for concern?

Suggested Listening

1. Mussorgsky—*Pictures from an Exhibition*
2. Scriabin—Préludes, Op. 11
3. Rachmaninoff—Tableaux Études, Op. 33
4. Prokofieff—Sonata No. 3
5. Shostakovich—Sonata No. 2
6. Kabalevsky—Sonata No. 3

SUGGESTED ADDITIONAL LISTENING

1. SCRIABIN—Sonata No. 5 *Poem of Ecstasy*
2. RACHMANINOFF—Prelude, G♯ Minor, Op. 23, No. 12; Prélude, G Major, Op. 23, No. 6
3. PROKOFIEFF—Suggestion Diabolique
4. PROKOFIEFF—Toccata, Op. 11
5. PROKOFIEFF—Sonata No. 6
6. SHOSTAKOVICH—Prélude and Fugue, D♭ Major, Op. 87
7. SHOSTAKOVICH—3 Fantastic Dances
8. KABALEVSKY—Children's Pieces, Op. 27
9. KABALEVSKY—Sonatine, Op. 13
10. MEDTNER—*Fairy Tales*, Op. 20
11. BALAKIREV—*Islamey*

CHAPTER

9

The Nineteenth and Twentieth Centuries in France

When the late seventeenth and early eighteenth-century French composers ceased to produce their unique baroque and rococo harpsichord works, a large non-productive period ensued during which the harpsichord was discarded and the piano, if it was adopted, was used so little that there are no sets of compositions worthy of record.

THE COMPOSERS

César Auguste Franck

The first composer to be considered chronologically is César Auguste Franck (1822-1890). Properly speaking, he is not French but a Belgian from Liége who settled, as an organist, in Paris, and wrote a large quantity of justifiably discarded piano music early in his career. It was not until the last few years of his life that he returned to writing piano music. His two worthy and late piano compositions are influenced by his organ predilection to the point where they have the sound of transcriptions. They are a Prelude, Chorale, and Fugue, and a Prelude, Aria, and Finale. They are very discursive, long, meandering works which nonetheless reveal great beauty of harmony and melody, particularly of harmony with very much chromaticism or half-step progression and very poignant melodies. The sections are vague in form and are unified by thematic recurrence and transformation, culminating in a fugal setting of the recurrent material. This last refers to the Prelude, Chorale, and Fugue.

Camille Saint-Saens

Camille Saint-Saens (1835-1921) was one of music's most gifted prodigies. He had a French mind, keen, logical, intellectual, witty—and nonsentimental to the point where he viewed everything emotional in art with suspicion. His piano works reveal this trait, and are unsatisfying. Very few are heard now and those are performed almost exclusively by French artists out of national pride. He fared best in études, preludes, and fugues, his smooth and facile piano concerti, and his famous set of variations for two pianos on a Beethoven theme. His work reveals a polish and facility which has been termed glib and his aversion to emotional qualities has robbed his music of enduring satisfaction. His humorous 2-piano and orchestral *Carnival of the Animals* will, however, probably outlast more serious works of greater composers since we have so little genuine and clever humorous music.

PREIMPRESSIONISM

Gabriel Urbain Fauré

Gabriel Urbain Fauré (1845-1924) may surely be called the greatest nineteenth-century French composer. A late discovery outside of France, he is becoming ever more respected and admired. True French preimpressionism is evident in his work. There is a kind of subtlety, particularly harmonically, which is infinitely more delicate than any German composer might have desired. There is a thinning of texture and a revealment of emotional nuance which must be called French since its like has never been heard elsewhere. There is a simplicity which is disarming and which conceals calculation only to be revealed on close study. He wrote a substantial quantity of piano pieces, Barcarolles, Nocturnes, Impromptus, Waltz-Caprices, and Preludes, many of each. Fauré's experiments harmonically are not easily discerned; one is somehow aware of sounds which differ from the customary ones.

Since he was a teacher of Ravel, we may say that he remotely fathered the great French Impressionist school. He did not influence it as did Erik Satie, but he doubtless engendered in Ravel a desire and love for delicacy of tonal variety and the belief that understatement can have as profound an effect as a great Wagnerian utterance in the manner of his Valhallic gods. Since Fauré's restrained understatement meets with mid-twentieth-century taste, he is constantly being studied now, performed ever more and recordings of his entire piano repertoire have appeared, placing him in a position almost coequal with his musical descendants, Ravel and Debussy.

IMPRESSIONISM: DEBUSSY AND RAVEL

Usually, when we speak of a composer in nationalist terms, we mean that he has become imbued with his native musical culture, the peculiar scales and intervals used in folk songs and dances and the rhythms peculiar to his home area. With the two greatest French composers, this is not so. Neither Claude Achille Debussy (1862-1918) nor Maurice Ravel (1875-1937) revelled in French songs and dances of any province of their country. On the contrary, they were more affected by influences of other countries. Thus Debussy showed Javanese influence in Pagodes and Voiles simply through hearing a gamelan or Javanese ensemble at a Paris Exposition. Ravel, whose mother was a Basque from northwest Spain, wrote much music using Spanish ideas. In one of his *Miroirs,* the title, in Spanish, is *Alborada Del Gracioso* (Morning Serenade of a Jester). Debussy wrote, without ever having been in Spain, *Evening in Granada* and *El Puerto del Vino* (The Wine Port) a reference to a Spanish cafe pictured on a postcard. De Falla, famed Spanish composer, declared this latter an epitome of Spanish rhythm, mood, and sensibility.

Then what has made these two particularly French? It was not a peasant root source but a highly sophisticated artistic controversy which underlay their art, and through their partisanship the effort to represent their belief in music resulted in Impressionism in music, as Impressionism existed in painting and Symbolism in French poetry at the end of the nineteenth and beginning of the twentieth centuries. If this sophisticated approach to the musical art had an intellectual rationale, it nonetheless resulted in a new kind of romanticism, not an outward-leaning lavish tone-poem type of writing but a delicate inward probing of after-thoughts and after-feelings concerning a subject or title. There is always a kind of reminiscent savoring of thought and feeling, a kind of looking back in their music which, as in any pensive recall, is devoid of spontaneous and violent emotional turbulence. By the same token, this delineation from far off of detail results in a subtlety which is so unique in music that it has come to be thought distinctly French and has caused all music of this type, whether written by these composers or their innumerable imitators in other lands, to be called Impressionist.

Claude Achille Debussy

This music loosens still more the ties that bound it, in the classic period, to symmetrical phrases, motivic melodies, diatonic harmonies, and reiterated rhythm patterns. The music of Debussy is harmony-oriented; melody is relatively rare and fragmentary. Phrases have vague boundaries since melodies are vague, and for the most part are engagingly assymetrical. Rhythm is usually somewhat undefined and motives, when used, are not repeated nearly enough to lend a rhythmic stamp to more than a small section of a piece. Harmonies do not, in their progression, stay long enough in one key to enable one to name the scale and there is a predilection in the music of both Debussy and Ravel for the older scales or modes of the sixteenth century and earlier. The form of the short character pieces is usually binary (AB) or ternary (ABA), though many pieces like Debussy's *Delphic Dancers* or Ravel's *Sad Birds* are simply composed by stringing ideas of similar mood together, in what is called through-composition, letting the first musical idea suggest the second, which in turn suggests a third, until the piece culminates and comes to an end.

Both Debussy and Ravel were principally piano composers though both wrote felicitously for the voice, small and large instrumental ensembles, and Ravel is considered one of history's greatest orchestrators. Debussy's experimental bias led him into considerably more harmonic variety than Ravel; he did not have Ravel's innate love of logic and so is far less incisive. He had no basic love for virtuoso technique and, with the exception of about six piano pieces, sheered away from pianistic bravado. The exceptions are the Toccata from the *Suite For Piano,* the wonderful *Joyous Island,* the *Fireworks* from the second Prelude volume, and perhaps three of the Études. Most of the Études are studies in sonorities, touch, and dynamics. Relatively few of Debussy's piano pieces have been discarded. A few youthful works are no longer played, occasional pieces from one or other of his sets are avoided but by far the greater number are eagerly learned and enjoyably performed.

He wrote two volumes of Preludes, the first of which is by far the more popular, though one wonders whether the popularity is that much more deserved. The pieces in the first volume tend to be shorter and far more traditional melodically, harmonically, and phrase-wise. This probably accounts also for their popularity. The moods evoked in the first volume are generally simple and the titles are sufficiently evocative to help greatly in their appreciation. The *Delphic Dancers* has the measured sinuous step of a priestly mystery, *Veils* (or Sails is an alternate translation of Voiles) is a misty whole-tone scale double note study begging for pedal blurring, returning to the sunlight sharply in a pentatonic chord-crashing interlude, only to sink into misty obscurity. The *Wind On The Plain* moans and whirs like a spinning wheel and shouts briefly like a gale. The *Sounds and Perfumes*

Revolving in the Evening Air has enchantingly subtle chord progressions and sudden little cascades of falling notes. *Footsteps in the Snow* is a picture of melancholy and desertion. *What the West Wind Saw* is a tempest which mutters and roars. The *Interrupted Serenade* is a travesty which indicates the difficulty of serenading and strumming on a too busy thoroughfare. And so it goes with variety and grace through both books. At times the composer presents a picture sufficiently objective to make one doubt his actual impressionism which should be more concerned with his reaction to the object of his inspiration rather than attempting to delineate the object itself. But by and large he is truly impressionistic and in pieces like *Goldfish* or *Reflections in the Water,* there is a truly subjective evocation to make one sigh with satisfaction at the authenticity of this artistic concept.

Debussy wrote two sets of Images, of which *Goldfish* is one piece and his beautiful *Evening in Granada* another. The latter is a muted far-off slow dance with, at times, only the rhythm enunciated in a way to remind one of the Cheshire Cat's smile after the Cat had disappeared, and with suggestions of popular melody fragments which never quite complete themselves. The *Goldfish* has similar fragments swirling in a musical liquid with so much color that it takes little imagination to evoke the iridescence of darting scaled fins. His *Joyous Island,* starting with a spinning trill and cascades of figuration, races from start to culmination to a variety of gay rhythms and harmonies until it arrives at a frenzied climax and ends as it began, coming full circle. The Sarabande from the Suite for the Piano treads an exquisitely slow and modal measure. All of his pieces give the pianist the joy of seeking tonal and pedal solutions to their problems; they are, for the most part, not difficult for the fingers but leave to the performer's imagination a variety of choices in their fulfillment. Small wonder that so many of his piano works are beloved of musician and general public.

Erik Satie

Before we turn to Ravel, a word should be said about a composer who, inconsequential in himself, may have been of great service to both the impressionist greats. He was Erik Satie (1866-1925), a self-taught dilettante who would have been a fit subject for any psychiatrist. He wrote a kind of music midway between Fauré and Debussy, sparsely scored, fragmentary, ruminative, and vague enough to qualify him as an early impressionist. He seemed under a compulsion to wryly view himself as a misfit and failure and poked fun at himself in entitling his music, such as Pieces in The Form Of A Pear, Cold

Pieces, Sports and Diversions, etc. He dedicated works to himself. His music is singularly static, without movement, like a still life or a tableau. He was the first of the "neo" composers, reaching back in time to write a modernized version of ancient slow dances like sarabandes and striving to picture even more ancient Greek models. He has been called a catalyst who, by his influence and suggestion, caused Debussy to return to the past, as well as Ravel, to use ancient modes and think in ancient styles.

Maurice Ravel

Thus Ravel wrote the *Tomb of Couperin,* a suite of pieces based on baroque styles. The effort resulted in a most beautiful set which reveals an admixture of the old and the new. The harmonies of the Prelude and its register compass belie the old but mix it delightfully with the new. The fugue is a most intricate example, using modality, of the devices common to the masters of this baroque style. He inverts the theme, overlaps it (called stretto), plays it in inversion against itself and in stretto at the same time. This ingenuity somehow is not rewarded by appreciation save by the performers who are in awe at this apparent erudition and who work so hard to encompass its articulation difficulties. *The Forlane,* a version of an old lilting Italian dance, is graced with exquisite dissonant harmonies and is so delicate that one never tires of hearing it, and it leaves the listener longing for it to continue indefinitely. The *Rigaudon* is robust and racy, with an ostinato B section whose lilting and simple melody sounds like a shepherd's pipe heard from afar. Ravel loved minuets and the one in this suite is a perfect example of his preference for this gentle treading dance. Like so much of his music, it reveals an exquisiteness of taste which makes one realize that he did not know the meaning of vulgarity or even earthiness. As in much romantic period music, this dance is in ABA form and his return to the A is again marked by his high manipulative technique wherein the B theme shows no sign of abatement but continues unchecked, while the A theme is superimposed on it. The suite ends surprisingly with a toccata, but this, despite its baroque title, turns out to be the nineteenth-century type, a long and driving perpetual-motion étude, magnificent in its working-out but somehow anachronistic when considered stylistically with the rest of the suite.

Ravel wrote most of his pieces in suite form but not with the intention of having each set uninterruptedly performed. Thus his *Miroirs* contains five pieces of which three are typically very fine. His *Night Moths,* The *Morning Song of A Buffoon,* and his *Sad Birds* are masterpieces. The others, *A Boat On The Ocean* and *Valley of the Bells,* are good enough but do not rival the first three. His greatest piano works are contained in his 3-piece suite *Gaspard de la Nuit,* inspired by the prose poetry of Louis Bertrand (1807-1842). The first, *Ondine,* treats of the legendary water spirit that falls in love with a mortal youth and, failing to lure him into the water, lashes herself into a fury and sinks beneath the waves. In this piece, Ravel reveals his admiration and emulation of Franz Liszt, as he builds figures to depict the shimmer of water with moon rays glancing from an infinitude of wavelets, and surrounds the plaintive call of the Ondine with marvelous passages in scales, arpeggios, broken chords, double notes, and polyrhythms. The second piece, the *Gibbet,* depicts in true impressionist style a corpse spinning slowly on a gallows and silhouetted in the rays of the setting sun. A single reiterated note in a melancholy rhythm pattern permeates the entire piece, while tragically dark chords using the hollow sound of open fifths lend a doomsday air to the scene. The harmonies are eerie and highly evocative. The last piece, Scarbo, succeeds in portraying the flashing antics of a kind of poltergeist that moves too fast to be seen. The debt to Liszt is again apparent in the fantastically difficult passages of repeated tones, perpetual motion figures, flashing arpeggios, and strange dissonances. These three pieces undoubtedly represent his finest achievement on the keyboard and it is only by virtue of the piano's development to its highest pitch of perfection that justice can be done to them.

A COMPARISON

Ravel has been called far more classic than Debussy. Where Debussy eschewed precise phrases, Ravel sought them. Debussy viewed form as constricting; Ravel felt most comfortable when confining his inspiration within formal limits. Ravel wrote a Sonatine in strictest form; Debussy wrote nothing that formal and even his violin sonata has not the classic structure. Ravel revealed his harmonic predilections in one of his earliest works, *Jeaux d'Eau* (The Fountain). He bases his harmonic scheme on an evolutionary premise rather than a revolutionary one, by simply building his chords to encompass more thirds. Thirds are the building blocks of traditional harmony; put two atop one another and you have a triad; superimpose another third and you have a seventh chord. Ravel superimposes yet another to make the chord of the ninth, and often another to make an eleventh. Debussy is not so simple. He often uses simple triads but is careful to make their sequence such that they frequently are unable to be classified as a group within the framework of one key. His chordal combinations are not as logical nor do they follow formulae. Both composers use the old modes; both indulge in polytonality or the usage of two (or more) keys simultaneously. Debussy follows the example of Chopin in his passage work though the end result is far from his model. Ravel admired Liszt and though his technical figuration is not Liszt's, it is not difficult to see the relationship.

THE SIX

In the twentieth century, two successive groups dominated the musical scene. One group was termed "The Six" and three of these composers attained prominence, though not as exceptional composers for the keyboard. They are Arthur Honegger (1892-1955), Darius Milhaud (born 1892), and Francis Poulenc (1899-1963). The three who are remembered more because they were group members than for their attainments are Georges Auric (1899-   ), Germaine Tailleferre (born 1892), and Louis Durey (born 1888). Of the famous three, only Poulenc and Milhaud wrote substantial quantities of piano music.

Arthur Honegger

Honegger's piano repertoire consists of little serious music, an early Toccata and Variations, and less than twenty more short works. The pieces are clean, clear, and to the point; like all of the Six, he was anti-impressionist and wrote with an almost exaggerated clarity and simplicity, a bit acerbic in harmony but not dissonant in the sense of the already emerging 12-tone school. His piano works are not performed as being inconsequential and have had no effect on the course of keyboard history.

Darius Milhaud

Darius Milhaud has written voluminously for the piano, as he has written largely for almost everything instrumental and vocal. He has had the peculiarly sponge-like ability to absorb all the atmospheres he has inhabited. Thus his *Rembrances* (Saudades) of Brazil in two books reflect the flavor of that country, with particular emphasis on Rio de Janeiro city subdivisions. The rhythms are spicy and local; the tunes are similar to popular ones of the area and the harmonies are traditional but piquantly flavored with wry dissonances and sudden excursions into polytonality. He has written similarly about Madrid in a three-piece suite, *Autumn,* and even three *Rag-Caprices* about a phase of American jazz. There is a reference to his ethnic ancestry in one of his late opuses, *The Seven-Branched Candelabra* of seven pieces. There are other late short works and even earlier lengthy works comprising two sonatas, a suite, variations, etc. Milhaud has done much experimentation with metres, rhythms, harmony, and form. He has been accused of writing over-prolifically. The accusation is a familiar one—too fast composition makes the quality suffer since not enough time has been taken to refine or discard inferior measures. It is difficult, this close to his time, to evaluate his work completely, but there may indeed be some validity in the accusation.

Francis Poulenc

Poulenc suffers from a sense of humor. Where Beethoven's humor was Jovian, Poulenc seems to continually deride himself gently in his music. It is rarely profound, always clever and frequently unexpected in turns of harmony and phrasing. He wrote bountifully for the piano but from his three *Perpetual Movements,* through his Cycles and suites of short pieces, there is a sameness of pianistic approach which marks him as limited in concept, adroit in technique, graceful instead of emotionally moving, and "toujours gai." This means that a small measure of his music can always be enjoyed as a diversion. He writes thinly to the point of emanciation, rather tenderly and a wee bit sentimentally at times, but then one senses his tongue in his cheek. His harmony is spicy but traditional and his pieces are frequently as little as one page in length. His two books of *Improvisations* are very representative of his musical outlook. It is a kind of French salon music with slightly jazzy references. His most noted work is entitled *Evenings In Nazelles.* It consists of eight variation portraits (of friends) preceded by a Preamble and followed by a Cadenza and Finale. Like all his music, the portraits are humorous, jazzy at times, simple and surprising in their quirks, and unexpected departures from the usual.

YOUNG FRANCE

France is a country of "movements." The Six movement ran its course unproductively and has been replaced by "Young France," a noncynical, nonhumoristic group professing rebellion against society's drift to mechanistic principles. They represent a return to Humanism, in essence another facet of Romanticism.

Andre Jolivet

One composer, André Jolivet (born 1905), finds his inspiration in primitivism and his music has preponderant rhythmic and percussive qualities. His suite *Mana* portrays a mystic energy flowing into what Messiaen (to be discussed) calls "our familiar fetishes" in an introduction. The titles of the pieces are *Beaujolais, The Bird, Bali Princess, The Goat, The Cow, Pegasus*. He has also written less interesting sonatas. He utilizes the 12-tone technique originating with Arnold Schoenberg which will be referred to in a following chapter.

Oliver Messiaen

Oliver Messiaen, (born 1908), probably represents the most powerful influence in France of his generation. Primarily an organist, he has still written substantially for the piano. He is one of the most intellectual composers who has ever lived and he blends this attribute of mind with deep religious feeling, a love of nature (particularly associated with the calls of birds), and a completely organized artistic aestheticism. Within this framework, he blends every modern scale and ancient mode, East Indian scales and rhythms and 12-tone elements. His organization is enormously complex and intellectually categorized so that every rhythm as well as every scale, every deviation from exactitude, can be labeled. Unless the music-desiring public is willing to undergo some intensive education, it will only appreciate his work on a directly romantic level, which is not necessarily wrong, since he aims primarily for passionate utterance. He is most regarded for his *Twenty Contemplations On The Infant Jesus*, a long, long work with explanations, and using very many old and new technical devices. It was published in 1944.

Pierre Boulez

His pupil, Pierre Boulez (born 1926), has carried complexity to a limit which strains at the mind. His rhythms are so complex as to defy exact rendition or comprehension. He is a 12-tonalist, using the technique in ways which are probably clear to him alone. His three sonatas are attempted by pianists who most frequently have to guess at his intentions since they are impossible to define clearly. He is, nonetheless, the most noted composer in France today.

Jean Françaix

Jean Françaix, (born 1912), is a paragon of simplicity by comparison with Boulez. A thorough disciple of the great French teacher and composer, Nadia Boulanger, he is neoclassic in outlook. His *Five Portraits of Young Girls* reproduces in modern guise the late seventeenth-century French Couperin-type of musical portrait, written almost as sparingly as his models but with contemporary sounds, harmonies, and intervals. He has a graceful Sonata which is in reality a Suite, comprising a Prelude, Elegie, Scherzo, and Toccata, and another grotesque harpsichord suite, *The Insectarium.* He writes a neogallant music which never strives for profundity but evokes the light touch in wit and humor and at times a gentle melancholy and tenderness.

SUGGESTED READING

Bauer, M. *Twentieth Century Music.* New York: Putnam, 1947, Chapter 10 (Impressionistic Methods); pp. 231-238 (Satie and The Six).

Collaer, P. *A History of Modern Music,* (trans. by S. Abeles). New York: Grosset & Dunlap, Inc., 1961, pp. 156-179 (The French aesthetic character).

Demuth, N. French Piano Music. Museum Press, Ltd. pp. 41-48 (Franck); 78-84 (Fauré); Chapter 7 (Romanticism and Impressionism); pp. 115-117 (The Six); Chapter 10 (Young France).

Gillespie, J. *Five Centuries of Keyboard Music.* Belmont, Calif.: Wadsworth Publishing Co., Inc., 1965, pp. 292-307 (19th-century composers); pp. 328-343 (Debussy and Ravel); pp. 366-373 (20th-century France).

Hansen, P. S. *An Introduction to 20th-Century Music.* Boston: Allyn & Bacon, Inc., 1961, pp. 11-43 (Debussy and Ravel); Chapters 7 and 8 (The Six and The Three).

Jean-Aubry, G. *An Introduction to French Music.* London: Palmer and Hayward, 1917, pp. 69-84 (Debussy).

Kirby, F. E. *A Short History of Keyboard Music.* New York: The Free Press, 1966, pp. 354-359 (Franck); pp. 380-392 (Debussy, Ravel, Satie); 393-396 (The Six).

Machlis, J. *Introduction to Contemporary Music.* New York: W. W. Norton & Company, Inc., 1961, pp. 110-143 (Impressionism); Chapter 4 (Away from Impressionism); pp. 435, 436 (Boulez).

SUGGESTED WRITTEN ASSIGNMENTS

1. To what extent was keyboard music composed in France from the end of the Rococo period until the middle of the nineteenth century?
2. Who is the first great French composer of keyboard works to point the way to the Impressionist school and how did he do so?
3. Erik Satie was important but not necessarily for the beauty of his writing. Why?
4. How is Impressionism an offshoot of Romanticism?
5. Why would the piano of the year 1800 have been unfit to play impressionist music?
6. What links with the past did the impressionist composers preserve and what did they discard?
7. What are the salient differences in the keyboard writing of Debussy and Ravel?
8. How did the composers like The Six manifest their rebellion against impressionism?

SUGGESTED LISTENING
1. FRANCK—Prélude, Chorale and Fugue
2. SAINT-SAËNS—Etudes
3. FAURÉ—Nocturne No. 2, B Major
4. DEBUSSY—Prélude *The Interrupted Serenade;* Prelude *Feux d'Artifices*
5. RAVEL—*Gaspard de la Nuit*
6. POULENC—*Improvisations*

SUGGESTED ADDITIONAL LISTENING
1. MILHAUD—*The Seven-Branched Candelabra*
2. MESSIAEN—Nine Meditations
3. FRANÇAIS—Concertino for Piano and Orchestra
4. HONEGGER—Concertino for Piano and Orchestra
5. FRANCK—Symphonic Variations for Piano and Orchestra
6. FAURÉ—Barcarolle in F sharp Minor, Op. 66; Theme and Variations, Op. 73
7. POULENC—Toccata; *Les Soirées de Nazelles*
8. RAVEL—*Le Tombeau de Couperin; Miroirs*
9. DEBUSSY—*Isle Joyeuse; Poissons d'or; Reflets dans l'Eau*

10

The Nineteenth and Twentieth Centuries in Hungary, Italy, England, Holland, and Scandinavia

HUNGARY: BARTÓK AND NATIONALISM

While it is virtually impossible to assess a composer's reputation in the grand process of history until many years have passed (one authority gives a minimum of 50 years), there have been isolated cases wherein composers have been quickly evaluated for greatness and accorded the recognition they deserve, either in their lifetimes or shortly thereafter. Bela Bartók (1881-1945) was so unfortunate as to die only a very short time before the fame he earned was extended to him. The greatest of all Hungarian composers, he brought nationalism in music to its highest possible eminence, and internationalism (in his chamber and orchestral works) to its greatest expression. Referring to his considerable pianistic prowess, it is somewhat surprising that he did not take the time to write more for the keyboard. All his work in this idiom is strongly folk-oriented, either in the shape of traditional national dances, or with themes and harmonies suggested by folk song.

There are Rondos on Hungarian Folk Tunes and Improvisations on Hungarian Peasant Songs. There are also Rumanian Folk Dances and Rumanian Christmas Songs. His interest in folk material was a direct result of field trips into the countryside where he collected and collated thousands of songs and dances witnessed and heard in remote villages where tradition had preserved a vast unspoiled art. From these sources Bartók derived many elements which can be listed as his tools-in-trade in piano writing.

The use of ostinato or short repeated bass pattern is one. This is also transferred to the melody, where short insistent motives repeat for many measures, varied at times by changing emphasis on different beats. The rhythms in his rapid pieces have a propellant, driving force which stamps them as primitive in concept. His harmonic palette is enormously colored, ranging from the simplest to the most complicated and dissonant chords, using a great variety of scales often tinged with orientalism. When he is not writing in a subdued, lyrical vein, he treats the piano as a percussive instrument, hammering his chords and rhythmic note groups in a way that has led many to embrace enthusiastically this purely twentieth-century concept of the instrument as primarily percussive. This contrasts sharply with the nineteenth-century view which endeavored to make the piano as lyrical sounding an instrument as possible. Since the advent of Bartók, the piano sound has been percussive in the writing of very many twentieth-century composers. A further trademark in Bartók's music is a kind of recitative, an improvisatory "parlando" or speaking style without clear rhythm or evenly balanced length of phrase. This is confined to his slower, introspective writing.

With all the above in his favor, it seems somewhat heretical to be forced to list his shortcomings. He wrote only one piece of length, a Sonata which has been neglected. This has puzzled many writers who find it hard to believe that what they term a masterpiece may be avoided because it is not a good piece, or should we say one that is not successful in performance. The defects inherent in his piano style are magnified whenever any piece or movement of a sonata is extended. The extreme shortness of his motives, frequently four or five rapid evenly-rhythmic notes in length, render it well-nigh impossible for him to develop them as musical ideas. After 40 or 50 repetitions and variations of a motive, no matter how ingeniously contrived and harmonized, the listener becomes impatient for something else. Anything else which is then presented, if similar to the first motive, must make for monotony. Anything very different must give an episodic quality to the larger entity embracing both motives. If Bartók realized this, then he was wise to avoid any other piano work of length, and made his suites stand in their stead. There are two of them. One, Opus 14, features the typical ostinato and driving elements in the two middle movements and a gay and slightly drunken sounding opening movement, and a sustained lyric closing movement whose disonances are fine examples of his unvaryingly good harmonic taste. The other suite, *Out-Of-Doors,* has five titled movements, fast and percussive in the first and last, an undulant *Barcarolle,* a drone piece, and a folk representation in the style of a nocturnal piece.

It is in another aspect of piano composition that Bartók is very important. In the twentieth century, music departed radically in sound from the nineteenth or eighteenth century traditional sounds. This created a gap in the education of those learning piano music, since there were no simple miniatures of the "modern" product for them to study as musical pathways leading in the desired direction of familiarity and understanding. Bartók undertook this task, not by writing a simple album of children's pieces in the nineteenth-century manner of Schumann and Mendelssohn, but on an unprecedented scale. Included in his works for children are one volume of Ten Easy Pieces, four volumes entitled *For Children,* containing 85 pieces, eighteen more pieces in his The First Term of the Piano, and nine Little Piano Pieces. As if this were not enough, he finally issued six new volumes entitled *Mikrokosmos,* containing 153 pieces in educationally progressive series, from one-or-two-line works to very complicated examples at the end. What is most remarkable is the exacting and uncompromising taste in the compositions; he never tried to make the simplest examples sound like Mozart or Schumann with diatonic or simple eighteenth-century chord progressions, but instead hewed rigorously to his purpose of accustoming the child's ear to new combinations of sounds, metres, and rhythms. All the scales and modes are explored, two keys presented simultaneously (bitonality), tone cluster (groups of contiguous half steps heard simultaneously), and harmonics. Syncopation, alternating metres by measures, and nationalistic dance examples from Hungary, Rumania, Bulgaria, Yugoslavia and even Bali are to be found here. Most contrapuntal devices, canon, ground, inversion, etc. are included. The service he has rendered to the young pianists and their teachers is inestimable and adds to the depth and luster of his great reputation.

CZECHOSLOVAKIA: MARTINU

Among the twentieth-century Czech composers who succeeded Smetana and Dvorák, only one can be cited here for his pronounced piano output. This is Bohuslav Martinu (1890-1959). The long line of nationalistic composers influenced mainly by their folk song and dance heritage has been strongly maintained in Czechoslovakia, and Martinu has adhered to this concept. He has incorporated other influences into his music, however, mainly French and, to a much smaller degree, American. This has resulted in a more international flavor than one would normally expect in a product of the Bohemian school of composition. He has a greatly developed and highly sophisticated technique of idiomatic writing for the keyboard; his music is difficult but feasible for good technicians; his writing contains a mixture of tonality and bitonality resulting in successive passages sounding variously sophisticated and naïvely folk-like. It is questionable, however, whether the emotional content of his music is sufficiently profound to give him a timeless reputation. He has written preludes, dances, études, a sonata, and various character pieces. He is popularly regarded as a neoclassicist despite his emergence from a romantically oriented school, because of the outside influences mentioned earlier and because of the sophistication evident in his skilled use of motive and key. It would still be difficult, however, to categorize him in this simple manner.

ITALY

Ferruccio Busoni

The first Italian composer who showed promise in his piano music was Ferruccio Busoni (1866-1924). He was a stunning pianist, possessed a towering intellect, and sadly, only an average compositional gift. Though he strove to free himself and music from traditionally romantic German shackles, he was only partially successful. He wanted to be a neoclassic composer, returning to the objectivity of his adored Bach and early Italian baroque composers, with the leavening afforded by the new harmonic, motivic, and rhythmic devices, and the enlarged keyboard technique. As might be expected, his rather large catalog of piano pieces reveals his breadth of intellectual outlook. His use of counterpoint is masterful, his harmony is often jagged. He wrote early romantic-type character pieces like those of Schumann, preludes like Chopin's, études dedicated to Brahms, transcriptions like Liszt's, and variations on a theme of Chopin. Later he wrote impressionist pieces, then pieces based on American Indian themes; still later and finally, highly contrapuntal works in dance style and baroque prelude and fugal style, using Bach themes to build large-scale fantasies and contrapuntal studies.

Gian Francesco Malipiero

Gian Francesco Malipiero, (born 1882), has written substantially for the piano. The early works are impressionist, stemming from Debussy, the later works are neobaroque, bearing the imprint of Bach and the early seventeenth-century Italian composers. Two pieces are homage works, the earlier to Debussy, the later to Bach. He has preludes and fugues and uses medieval church chant in at least one late work, *The Preludi, Ritmi Canti Gregoriani.*

Goffredo Petrassi

Goffredo Petrassi (born 1904), has written a set of clever Inventions and a Toccata for the Keyboard, quite idiomatic, not too difficult, and enjoyable, if not profound. He illustrates an Italian quality of lyricism which pervades most pieces by this country's composers, no matter what idiom and what schools they embrace.

Luigi Dallapiccola

Another such innate lyricist and possibly the best known of Italy's piano composers is Luigi Dallapiccola (born 1904). It is not the quantity but the quality of his piano writing which has brought him to the forefront of piano recognition by performers and composers. An American-sponsored work, the *Notebook of Annalibera* (his daughter) has been adjudged one of this century's finest musical efforts. It is a suite of eleven pieces written in an illustrious combination of the 12-tone series with baroque contrapuntal examples such as canon (works of various types of strict imitation). Though he uses these intellectual elements, the results are beautiful musical examples, very lyric, clear if subtle rhythms, highly varied, and imaginative in keyboard device use. They are difficult to play well, but so rewarding that they receive far more performances than many twentieth-century compositions which are not as difficult.

ENGLAND

England's nineteenth century paralleled Italy's in at least one respect, that of revealing next to no piano interest. This has lasted almost to the present and it is only within recent years that significant piano music has begun to flourish. Before that composers like John Ireland (1879-1963), Frank Bridge (1879-1941), Sir Arnold Bax (1883-1953), Cyril Scott (born 1879), and Lennox Berkeley (born 1903) wrote small character pieces in a purely romantic and quite superficial vein. Michael Tippett (born 1905) is in the forefront of the new composers who, inspired by a young generation of unusually fine keyboard performers, have begun to write works worthy of their pianistic ability. His *Sonata No. 2* in one movement exploits most of the traditional piano virtuoso devices, in contrast to his Sonatina written, except for the last movement, with great restraint.

HOLLAND: PIJPER

Holland is indeed fortunate in having governmental encouragement of its composers. The result, while happy for other forms of music making, has had relatively little effect on the keyboard, since few composers have found it a congenial idiom. The most prominent and certainly the widest known has been Willem Pijper (1894-1947) who, in a highly imaginative manner and backed by solid intellectual ability, has written three Sonatinas, a Sonata, and various short works. In these good keyboard pieces, he has used bitonality, varied rhythms, metres, and even polymetres, resulting in a product far more interesting than shocking. In his work there is revealed an admirable clarity of construction and fine musical taste.

His pupil, Henk Badings (born 1907), has written many lengthy sonatas in a partial neoclassic style. He is enough of an individualist to have preserved his own concepts, though the heavier-textured influence of Reger and Hindemith may be discerned in his work.

NORWAY: GRIEG

Scandinavia must be represented, to begin with, by its only major piano composer, the Norwegian Edvard Grieg (1843-1907). This purely nationalist-romantic composer, having studied in Germany and having become absorbed in the Schumannesque tradition, early asserted his interest in the music and poetry and dance of the northland. Though his two large-scale piano works, his Sonata in e minor and Ballade in g minor, are very lightly touched by nationalist influence (a folk song is the basis for variations in the Ballade), his next major work, a suite, is entitled *From Holberg's Time*. Following this, he delved deeply into his homeland's music, ferreting out the characteristic rhythms of the dances, the melodic intervals of their odd scales, and the harmonies, basically simple yet sufficiently different to stamp them as of national origin. He then wrote a very large number of short pieces, *Humoresque, Album Leaves, Norwegian Dances, Pictures From the People's Lives, Norwegian Mountain Tunes, Norwegian Folk Melodies, Lyrical Pieces* and finally the *Slatter*, 17 folk dances.

Because he wrote essentially simple music, he is not performed on the concert stage (save for his Concerto) but has remained popular in the home and has provided a welcome addition to the intermediate age teaching repertoire.

DENMARK: NIELSEN

The Danish composer, Carl Nielsen (1865-1931), like Sibelius, did not concentrate on the keyboard, but what he wrote was far more substantial than Sibelius' piano works and far more rewarding. His work is ostensibly neoclassic, a Chaconne, Variations, two suites, and various short pieces. But his tonal palette is so richly hued and his piano idiom sufficiently virtuosic to assert a subjectivity which gives his work a fine combination of classic and romantic elements and defies neat categorization.

SUGGESTED READING

Bauer, M. *Twentieth Century Music.* New York: G. P. Putnam's Sons, 1947, Chapter 11 (Overview of composers).

Collaer, P. *A History of Modern Music* (trans. by S. Abeles). New York: Grosset & Dunlap, Inc., 1961, Chapter 10 (Nationalism and eclecticism).

Gillespie, J. *Five Centuries of Keyboard Music.* Belmont, Calif.: Wadsworth Publishing Co., Inc., 1965, pp. 354-358 (Italy); pp. 347-376 (Hungary); pp. 377-379 (Holland); pp. 381-384 (England).

Hansen, P. S. *An Introduction to Twentieth-Century Music.* Boston: Allyn & Bacon, Inc., 1961, Chapter 12 (Bartók).

Kirby, F. E. *A Short History of Keyboard Music.* New York: The Free Press, 1966, pp. 415-424 (Bartók); pp. 436-442 (England, Poland, Italy).

Lockwood, A. *Notes On the Literature of the Piano.* Ann Arbor: University of Michigan Press, 1940, pp. 24, 25 (Bartók); pp. 45-47 (Busoni); pp. 95, 96 (Grieg).

Machlis, J. *Introduction to Contemporary Music.* New York: W. W. Norton & Company, Inc., 1961, pp. 183-191 (Bartók); pp. 239-241 (Busoni); pp. 246-254 (Czech, Dutch, English composers).

Salazar, A. *Music in Our Time.* New York: W. W. Norton & Company, Inc., 1946, p. 82 (Grieg); pp. 297-304 (Bartók).

SUGGESTED WRITTEN ASSIGNMENTS

1. Name at least six musical devices used repeatedly by Bartók.
2. What great service did Bartók render in the field of the child's musical education?
3. What are the shortcomings in Bartók's keyboard style?
4. How is the piano used in the twentieth century in comparison to the nineteenth century? How did Bartók contribute to this?
5. How did Martinu differ markedly from the school that fostered him?
6. Why has Grieg persisted in public esteem despite his condemnation at the hands of Shaw?
7. Why was piano composition neglected in Italy in the nineteenth century?
8. How have the composers of Holland been assisted?

SUGGESTED LISTENING

1. BARTÓK—Suite for Piano, Op. 14
2. SZYMANOWSKI—Mazurkas, Op. 50
3. GRIEG—Lyric Pieces, Op. 12, Op. 38, Op. 43
4. NIELSEN—Suite, Op. 45

SUGGESTED ADDITIONAL LISTENING

1. NIELSEN—Symphonic Suite, Op. 8, 3 Piano Pieces, Op. 59

2. Bartók—Sonatina for Piano; Sonata for Piano (1926); Rhapsody for Piano, Op. 1; Out of Doors; Sonata for Two Pianos and Percussion; Mikrokosmos; *Improvisations*, Op. 20
3. Busoni—Fantasia Contrappuntistica for Two Pianos; Piano Transcriptions of Bach
4. Kodály—9 Pieces for Piano (1910); 7 Piano Pieces, Op. 11
5. Bax—Mediterranean (1921)
6. Tcherepnin—Concerto No. 2 for Piano and Orchestra
7. Grieg—Sonata, Op. 7, E Minor

11

The Nineteenth and Twentieth Centuries in Spain

THE GOLDEN AGE OF SPANISH PIANISM

Spain is yet another country which enjoyed a pianistic awakening through the impetus provided by research and discovery in folk song and dance. Two minor composers deserve the credit for having instituted an investigation and subsequent classification of a large mass of Spanish folk music. They were Felipe Pedrell (1841-1922) and Federico Olmeda (1865-1909). Pedrell became the teacher of some of Spain's outstanding nationalist composers, who were thus awakened to this national treasury and used it to the glory of their country as well as themselves.

The piano is unusually well fitted for the revelation of Spanish musical elements. Technically, this music has two basic and contrasting qualities. One is the lyric sensuous melody, frequently modal, giving it an archaic and authentically regional character. The other consists of an enormous variety of rhythms, frequently superimposed upon each other, so that the listener is well-nigh hypnotized by a kind of rhythmic concatenation which traps him in its cross currents. The latter nineteenth-century Spanish composers wrote for the piano with such success that the last quarter of the nineteenth century and first decade of the twentieth century may be called a golden age of Spanish pianism. This type of piano writing is difficult to perform because of its antithetical combination of legato line and staccato rhythm.

THE COMPOSERS

Isaac Albéniz

Four composers shared in this nationalist awakening. The greatest, pianistically if not musically, was Isaac Albéniz (1860-1909). His compositional gift was as precocious as his pianistic one; early on, he composed for his concert appearances and shortly began to use Spanish native music as the basis for his piano compositions. He composed glibly, rapidly, in uneven bursts of taste. His output was enormous; a considerable amount was tawdry, but here and there appeared works of undeniable charm and musical worth. In the most ideal manner, he culminated his relatively short life with a truly magnificent set of pieces, twelve in all, which appeared in four sets of three pieces each, totally entitled *Iberia,* the ancient and timeless name for the Spanish peninsula.

These pieces are a diadem of Spanish piano music, very difficult to perform, as varied as the areas and peoples they grace in sound. Among the represented dance rhythms are the fandango, malaguena, paso-doble and seguidilla. Included are references to the port of Cadiz in the title *El Puerto* as well as the cities of Sevilla, Granada, Malaga, Jerez, and Madrid; also the province of Andalusia. The writing has uniformity only in its setting forth of song and rhythm and corus-cating figuration by way of repetition and variation of themes. The pieces are of unsurpassed brilliance and truly represent the greatest possible achievement in Spanish piano music.

Perhaps, if one might pick a favorite from this suite, the *Triana,* named for the glittering gypsy quarter of Seville, has not a single measure that is not imbued with brilliant and imaginative pianism. *Evocaçión* is beautifully atmospheric, while *El Albaicín* and *Eritaña* (an Inn), although repetitive, are most suggestive of those qualities sought after by a writer of descriptive music.

Enrique Granados

A second composer merits almost as much credit as Albéniz in re-vealing the Spanish musical heritage. He is Enrique Granados (1867-1916) whose life was tragically shortened when the ship on which he and his wife were traveling was torpedoed and sunk during the first World War. Another student of the famous Pedrell, he was con-sistent in his usage of Spanish materials but was considerably more romantic than Albéniz in his treatment of them. Far more subjective in his immersion in the Spanish sound, he writes more in the vein of the Russian composers who identified themselves completely with their native music.

He wrote a number of early dances using the same basic rhythms employed by Albéniz but simpler, usually less adorned with figuration and, it must be confessed, less interesting or sophisticated. Like Al-béniz, he was a pianist of concert caliber who pandered to public taste, writing some non-Spanish works of superficial brilliance, marches, waltzes, and an Allegro de Concert, as well as his dances and Spanish rhapsodies. Like Albéniz, he reserved his greatest inspiration for a grand suite, basing it on a series of sketches for tapestries by the great painter, Francesco Goya. They depict scenes from the lives of a peculiarly Spanish picaresque type, the Majos, wealthy and aristocratic young men and women of a period (eighteenth century) who disguised themselves as common people and sought adventure in the streets after dark. He called the suite *Goyescas,* and subtitled each piece of the six after the sketches. They are somewhat uneven in quality, and several suffer from inordinate length, having a meandering character which fails to arrive at a meaningful climax. Despite their shortcomings, they reveal many moments of transcendent beauty. The first, *the Gallants,* uses popular song themes. Several variations separated by refrains show his skillful use of embellishing figuration which is quite as good as that of Albéniz. His color sense leads him to constantly melting and differing harmonies and the themes are interwoven with shiftingly hued passages of extraordinary difficulty. At least two other pieces may be considered superb. One is the world famous *Maiden and the Nightingale,* wherein a maiden pours forth her lovesickness in the form of a plaint, and is answered by a bird-like cadenza. The music is unsurpassed in its richly emotional appeal. It may not be considered profound in the German sense, but it fills an emotional need recognized by every listener and never fails to stir response. The third piece to deserve the highest praise is the *Fandango of The Candle,* evocative in its monotonous rhythmic background, its slow languorous melody, and its ever more completely interwoven ornamental passages. Despite undeniably beautiful moments, the other three, *Conversation Through the Grill, Love And Death,* and *Epilogue* are less inspired.

Manuel de Falla

Manuel de Falla, (1876-1946), the third of the four, must be given space here since he, like Stravinsky in Russia, is perhaps Spain's most esteemed composer. The analogy is apt, because, like Stravinsky, he is not important for the piano. He wrote four early Spanish Pieces, not outstanding, but still redolent of native sounds and sights. Other than this set, there is only one piece, a somewhat primitive sounding *Fantasía Baetica,* jarring in dissonance, episodic and not successful musically. He is known for none of the above, but rather for his poor transcription of his *Ritual Fire Dance,* ballet music owing its transfer to the keyboard to the suggestion of his friend, the great pianist,

Artur Rubinstein. His greatest and almost fantastically beautiful piece is a composition for orchestra with what amounts to a piano obbligato or commentary, *Nights in The Gardens Of Spain,* a set of episodes or movements inspired by the *Alhambra* and written with such happy inspiration that it might stand with the greatest in all Spanish art.

Joaquin Turina

The fourth composer, Joaquin Turina (1882-1949) is far less gifted than the three already named. He, like the others, was both Spanish and French trained, and likewise, channeled his talent into his native idiom, resulting in some early extended works and later in short character pieces. The dance rhythms of provincial Spain are again heard; his melodies are, however, somewhat saccharine in their sentimentality and his harmony is very conventional. The result, while too good to be termed inferior music, does not compare with the music of Albéniz and Granados.

THE INTERNATIONALISTS

There is a new generation of composers now in Spain, young internationalists who have quite forsaken the folk roots of their fathers and like most of the western world have embraced the new techniques of 12-tone polytonality, quartal harmony, etc. Cristobal Halffter (born 1930) is the son of Ernesto Halffter, who was a Falla pupil. He has a Sonata and a much later Introduction, Fugue, and Finale. Others are Luis de Pablo (born 1930) and Manuel Carra (born 1931). These are extremists stemming from Webern and writing music as contemporary as any in Europe.

SUGGESTED READING

Chase, G. *The Music of Spain.* New York: Dover Publications, Inc., 1959, pp. 150-165 (Albéniz and Granados); pp. 182-197 (de Falla); pp. 175, 176 (Turina).

Collaer, P. *A History of Modern Music,* (trans. by S. Abeles). New York: Grosset & Dunlap, Inc., 1961, pp. 353-359 (de Falla and later composers).

Gillespie, J. *Five Centuries of Keyboard Music.* Belmont, Calif.: Wadsworth Publishing Co., Inc., 1965, pp. 315-326 (The Golden Age).

Kirby, F. E. *A Short History of Keyboard Music.* New York: The Free Press, 1966, pp. 433-436 (Spanish composers, 20th century).

Lockwood, A. *Notes on the Literature of the Piano.* Ann Arbor: University of Michigan Press, 1940, pp. 1, 2 (Albéniz); p. 94 (Granados).

Machlis, J. *Introduction to Contemporary Music.* New York: W. W. Norton & Company, Inc., 1961, pp. 259, 260 (de Falla).

Salazar, A. *Music in Our Time*. New York: W. W. Norton & Company, Inc., pp. 304-307 (National Music of Spain).

Suggested Written Assignments

1. To what did the late nineteenth-century renaissance of Spanish music lead pianistically?
2. What are the two contrasting characteristics of Spanish music?
3. What is Albéniz's greatest composition?
4. What are some of the Spanish dances used by Albéniz and Granados?
5. On what are the Goyescas by Granados based?
6. What is Albéniz's fault as a composer?
7. What has happened to nationalism in present-day Spain?

Suggested Listening

1. Albéniz—*Triana* from *Iberia*
2. Granados—"Maiden and the Nightingale" from *Goyescas*
3. de Falla—*Pièces Espagnoles* (4)
4. Turina—*Sevilla* (Suite)

Suggested Additional Listening

1. Albéniz—*Evocacion* from *Iberia; Navarra; El Puerto* from *Iberia*
2. Granados—*Danzas Españolas* (1900); *Los Requiebros* from *Goyescas; El Fandango del Candil* from *Goyescas*
3. de Falla—*Fantasia Baetica;* Ritual Fire Dance
4. Turina—*Contes d'Espagne*
5. Mompou—*Impresiones Intimas*
6. Espla—*Sonata Española*, Op. 53
7. Rodrigo, J.—*Danzas de España*

Germany in the Twentieth Century

The piano, so much the favorite home and concert instrument in the nineteenth century, has suffered a progressive concert decline in the twentieth century. It still remains, however, a favorite in the home. This has been reflected in the decreasing number of compositions written for it by reputable composers. Pieces by the late eighteenth and nineteenth-century composers in Germany numbered from the dozens to the hundreds; in the twentieth century, one can usually count on the fingers of the two hands the number of pieces composed by fine composers who truly represent the twentieth-century styles.

THE TRADITIONALIST

Paul Hindemith

In Germany, less than a half dozen outstanding composers have written substantially for the piano. First among these was Paul Hindemith (1895-1963). His production was so prolific that he brings the classic and baroque composers to mind. But this output has its piano limits. There are a few groups of early works, written when he was in his 20's and early 30's, entitled *In One Night* and Dance Pieces, some later Études and a "1922" Suite, redolent of jazz. Then he began to use his uniquely developed harmonic and contrapuntal style in the best possible way and in 1936 he issued three sonatas, each a masterwork.

Hindemith was a composer sufficiently old-fashioned to believe in tonality—that is to say, a scale basis and harmonies related to keys. To be sure, he often built chords in fourths (quartal harmony) and occasionally used two scales at once (bitonality) with their disparate harmonies heard simultaneously. He wrote linearly or contrapuntally at frequent intervals and his form is a fine adaptation of late and early eighteenth-century models. Thus he wrote in the most famous sonata, the third, a magnificent fugue for the last movement. One of the fugal themes had already appeared in the preceding or third movement in a short foretaste of things to come. The first movement uses a characteristic eighteenth-century rhythmic pattern very simply and repetitiously, ingeniously varied with other-voice figuration. The second movement adapts the late eighteenth-century scherzo concept with short sharp motives, offset by a drumming and running B section before a purely classic return to the first scherzo theme. The slower third movement has a tolling, booming sound with great rhythms like the crash of sea waves, interrupted by the aforementioned fugal fragment.

Besides these three significant sonatas, he composed a purely neobaroque work, clearly modeled on the well-known preludes and fugues of Bach and exploiting the various keys in much the same manner as its prototype. This is the *Ludus Tonalis*. It contains 12 fugues separated by Interludes, preceded by a Prelude, and closing with a Postlude. The Postlude is an intellectual curiosity since it represents every note of the prelude but played backward or retrograde. The fugues display his great scholarship and technique; the interludes modulate from the preceding fugue to the one following. The harsh fact is that only a few of the interludes are attractive and even fewer of the fugues, despite their high erudition. They are not very difficult, but significantly do not arouse enough interest for any but an extremely occasional performance.

DODECAPHONISM

Arnold Schönberg
The greatest influence on music of the twentieth century was exercised by Arnold Schönberg (1874-1951). Feeling that music was being led up a blind alley if composition continued along the Wagner-Strauss path, he terminated his own substantial and talented efforts in this direction, utilized the extreme chromaticism already permeating the Wagnerian strain, and went one step further, dispensing with key or scale completely. To fill the vacuum created by this action, he conceived a method of composition whereby each and every note of the 12-tone chromatic scale had equal significance. An arbitrary arrangement by the composer of these 12 pitches became a pattern to be

used in whole or in part, reversed, inverted, or both, and also susceptible of transposition or starting the pattern on a different pitch. With all the permutations and combinations of pattern and part-pattern, together with rhythm and register variation made possible by this method or technique, the composer could write with an exceptional internal unity wherein every note of the piece would have to be accountable and found within the original pattern. This is a typical Germanic intellectualization of a very high order, and its effect upon the world of composition, slow at first, grew to such dimensions that by mid-century, almost every composer of any age, old as well as young, had succumbed to composing with Schönberg's "twelve tones." The writing is basically linear or contrapuntal; there is a great similarity of sound in many 12-tone compositions since, in the zeal to avoid tonality, the intervals of diminished fifth or augmented fourth and minor ninth or minor second are used to an exhaustive degree.

EXPRESSIONISM

Schönberg wrote his three piano pieces, Op. 11, as a pre-essay while groping toward his finished 12-tone concept, then wrote three small keyboard pieces, Op. 19, while still experimenting. It was only in 1923, fifteen years after Op. 11, that he began, in the last of five keyboard pieces, to attain his "tone row" end and from then on he used his arbitrary arrangements of pitches with the utmost confidence and skill. The Op. 11 pieces are stunning works and tend to disprove his thesis that the best would be heard only when his theory had matured. They are expressionistic, as are all his works. This is to say that they are enormously emotional, so intense in projected feeling that each short group of measures in any piece tends to exhaust an emotional potential, requiring a musical about-face in tempo, rhythm, interval pattern, and mood in the following short measure group. Expressionism in his subsequent 12-tone works combines two extremes, the extreme of emotion with the extreme of compositional discipline. After its introduction and summary rejection by a public and its musicianly segment as being too "intellectual," too "mathematical," too "abstruse," and too "cacophonous," this technique of writing has seized the twentieth-century music creators in a well-nigh universal grip. Composers such as Stravinsky and Copland, Krenek, and a host of avant-garde Europeans and Americans, both North and South, and Japanese have taken second looks at the method of composition in 12 tones and have adopted it with varying degrees of enthusiasm. Other composers have used it at moments for effect and still others have modified it according to their personal inclination.

Schönberg wrote only brief pieces for piano, even when he strung several together in a kind of neobaroque suite with the various pieces entitled *Prelude, Gavotte with Minuet, Intermezzo* (not a baroque title), *Minuet with Trio and Gigue.* Again the flavor has an odd quality of extremes, using the by-now famous technique and intricate rhythms set in an almost stilted, archaic mold.

Besides this suite and the already mentioned Op. 11 pieces, he wrote a few sets of short piano pieces, five in Opus 23, two in Opus 33, and six very short spare pieces in Opus 19. Scarcely sufficient, one would think, to cause a great furor. It is too soon to say how his work affected composition for the piano. Probably adversely, if we count the piano works of subsequent 12-tone composers who, while not neglecting the piano entirely, have spent their efforts chiefly in other instrumental or vocal media. Many factors are present, not the least of which is the popularity pendulum which has swung away from the piano recital in favor of instrumental and vocal offerings.

Within the scope of a book as limited as this, we cannot hope to name more than a very few of the many contemporary German composers and must confine ourselves to those whose prominence is international rather than national.

Boris Blacher

Boris Blacher (born 1903) is known internationally, but, unlike Hindemith, played very little. If he is given prominence here, it is because he introduced a concept of organized metres which may be important in music's evolution. In a work entitled *Ornamente,* he writes a set of nine measures, each containing one more beat than its predecessor and then, in the next nine, subtracts one beat from each successive measure until he ends with what he has started. This is a simple plan which, in the pieces that follow, he greatly complicates but always with a mathematical formula of metres. It is a moot question whether anything of permanent value to music will result from this experiment. Generally, his music is lean, thinly voiced, and deliberately dry.

ALEATORIC MUSIC

Karlheinz Stockhausen

Schönberg is no longer a controversial figure and the palm has passed into the hands of Karlheinz Stockhausen (born 1928). The latest concept which has invaded the musical domain has the term "aleatoric," or chance or random selection. Stockhausen's music exploits this concept in diversified ways on the keyboard, leading to a kind of directed improvisation, not so much of notes as of choices of passages to be played with choices of tempo and dynamics. In this way, no piece might ever be played twice in the same manner. As usual, the term "music" has had to be redefined to fit the changing concepts, and for all but the young, there has been a reluctance to admit that Stockhausen's offerings, no matter how seriously meant, fit into a truly musical category.

Alban Berg

Mention should be made, briefly, of a Sonata, Op. 1, by Alban Berg (1885-1935) which is not a 12-tone work, though Berg was an ardent Schönberg disciple. This earliest published work is beautifully lush and quite tonal in the late Germanic tradition of emotional personalism. This is his only published work for piano.

Anton Webern

A similarity exists in the sole piano variations by Anton Webern (1883-1945). This is a serial (12-tone) work which, in Webern's incredibly spare, compact style, uses many contrapuntal devices, canon, mirror-canon, retrograde inversion, etc. It is a curious work, intense and disciplined, in which it is very difficult to trace the subject of the variations or its various metamorphoses. Webern is the springboard for much European writing today. Composers in Germany, France, and Italy feel they have continued in the path indicated by him.

Wolfgang Fortner

Wolfgang Fortner (born 1907) has written in various "neo" styles until his seven Elegies appeared, when it was evident that he had also succumbed to serialism (12-tone). The seven pieces are hardly elegies in the elegiac sense of gentle melancholy, but are intensely expressionistic and range in tempo to the highest speeds and loudest dynamics. They are most arresting and even very beautiful if surprising in view of their title. He is widely considered one of Germany's more important composers ranging outside of the aleatoric and electronic group. These latter composers use created sound electronically conceived and amplified or otherwise modified to again attain a goal which calls into argument the definition of music.

SUGGESTED READING

Collaer, P. A History of Modern Music (trans. by S. Abeles). New York: Grosset & Dunlap, Inc., 1961, Chapter 2 (Schönberg, Webern, Berg); pp. 312-326 (Hindemith); pp. 394-400 (Electronic music, Stockhausen).

Gillespie, J. *Five Centuries of Keyboard Music.* Belmont, Calif.: Wadsworth Publishing Co., Inc., 1965, pp. 348-354 (Expressionism).

Hansen, P. *An Introduction to Twentieth Century Music.* Boston: Allyn & Bacon, Inc., 1961, Chapters 10-13 (4 composers); pp. 389-391 (Stockhausen).

Kirby, F. E. *A Short History of Keyboard Music.* New York: The Free Press, 1966, pp. 401-405 (Hindemith, Blacher, Fortner); pp. 408-412 (Schönberg).

Machlis, J. *An Introduction to Contemporary Music.* New York: W. W. Norton & Company, Inc., 1961, pp. 334-352 (Atonality and Schönberg).

Salazar, A. *Music in Our Time.* New York: W. W. Norton & Company, Inc., 1946, pp. 203-210 (Schönberg); pp. 236-240 (12-Tone system).

Schönberg, A. *Style and Idea.* New York: Philosophical, 1950, Chapter 5 (Composition with 12 tones).

SUGGESTED WRITTEN ASSIGNMENTS

1. How does the quantity of piano music written by twentieth-century composers compare generally with the nineteenth century?
2. Why does Hindemith remind us of Bach?
3. Why did Schönberg change his style so radically?
4. Describe the use of pitch and row in 12-tone composition.
5. What effect has this new style had on other composers?
6. What is meant by aleatoric music?
7. What is meant by the term "expressionism" and what composer may be termed expressionistic?
8. What did Blacher innovate in music?
9. Does Berg's solo piano piece fall into the pattern of 12-tone music?

SUGGESTED LISTENING

1. HINDEMITH—Sonata, No. 3 (1936)
2. SCHÖNBERG—Three Piano Pieces, Op. 11
3. STOCKHAUSEN—11 Piano Pieces (1954-61)

SUGGESTED ADDITIONAL LISTENING

1. BERG—Sonata, Op. 1
2. WEBERN—Variations
3. SCHÖNBERG—Suite for Piano, Op. 25; Five Piano Pieces, Op. 23
4. HINDEMITH—Suite 1922, Op. 26

13

The Americas, North and South, Nineteenth and Twentieth Centuries

EUROPEAN TRADITIONS PERSIST

North American piano music began, as might be expected, with the direct importation of music and composers from Europe who transplanted their tradition but made no attempt to alter or supplant it for a lengthy period. Until the twentieth century, we cannot claim more than one composer who attempted to depict anything in his music which could be said to differ from European music or could even be favorably compared.

Louis Moreau Gottschalk

Much has been made of the music of Louis Moreau Gottschalk (1829-1869) because he incorporated folk music (dance rhythms, tunes, and harmonies) of negro, creole and Caribbean Indian origins into his compositions. Other than this, he wrote typically European type character pieces, with naïve titles like *The Last Hope, The Banjo, The Dying Poet, Death,* etc. In our zeal to establish an American tradition, we have fixed on him as on a foundation stone but an examination of his music makes him crumble like a weak support. The sad fact is that his music is shallow, unimaginative, and meaninglessly virtuosic. His taste is unrefined and present-day American musicians tend to be embarrassed by well-meant attempts to impose him on local and foreign audiences. His music reveals a dearth of harmonic variety; it is melodically saccharine or vulgarly "catchy" and one suspects that his representational folk music has been altered to pander to a much unfashioned public taste. This indictment is soberly and reluctantly made since the author would be very happy to announce or endorse a thoroughly gifted nineteenth-century native American.

Edward MacDowell

A composer who sincerely but unsuccessfully tried to be American in his music was Edward MacDowell (1861-1908). His training was thorough and thoroughly German to the extent where he could never depart from the ingrained central European tradition. It manifested itself in the titled character piece, the simple ABA form, the harmonic palette of his teacher, Joachim Raff, and the pianistic virtuosity stemming from Liszt. His "Americanism" consisted of somewhat feeble attempts to incorporate negro and Indian tunes. He wrote only for the piano or piano with other instruments in ensemble, and his output was voluminous.

There are several "sets" as distinguished from "suites" since the pieces of a set are not expected to be played continuously any more than Mendelssohn's *Songs Without Words*. The best known set is the *Woodland Sketches* since it contains *To A Wild Rose* and *To A Water Lily*. Probably the *Sea Pieces* represent some of his finest piano writing in miniature. *Fireside Tales* contains his *Br'er Rabbit*. His Twelve Études are difficult and certainly more rewarding musically than Czerny or Cramer but are a far cry from Chopin or Liszt. Late in life, he wrote four large-scale sonatas with extramusical titles, *Tragic* (commemorating Raff's death), *Eroica* (based on the King Arthur Legends), *Norse* (dedicated to Grieg and bearing a Valhalla implication), and *Keltic* (called by him a Bardic Rhapsody on a Gaelic subject). His music is permeated with quotations by contemporary and past poets as well as himself. His sonatas are never played; they are simply not worth the effort, though they are somewhat impressive melodramatically on first hearing. Probably his finest large-scale work is his second concerto, which is brilliantly pianistic and in which the orchestral color and pianistic interchanges substitute brilliance for profundity.

The above citation of just two American composers must not lead to the belief that there were no others. There were many, but their music has descended into oblivion, after a short period of popularity, and it would be a waste of time to list their many names and works. The many latter nineteenth-century composers wrote character pieces for the most part, watered versions of their beautiful Germanic counterparts with a weak leavening of American folk themes and rhythms. Since so many of these folk works were altered versions of European originals imported as much as a hundred or more years earlier, they might well have lent themselves to fine settings or have been used as a basis for charming character pieces. These minor composers were not steeped in this music, however, nor did they have the kind of talent possessed, for example, by the nationalistic Spanish composers. So, on the whole, they are better forgotten.

The tradition of European compositional study has never died in our country so that it has been difficult for us to develop a truly American tradition. That we have finally begun to succeed is a distinct credit to our composer class which has wanted to do this. As in most twentieth-century areas of the western world, composition has taken two paths—one nationalistic and the other internationalistic. The American composers have dipped into every historic dish. There are outright 12-tone composers (variously called atonalists, dodecaphonists, and serialists), composers who have used 12-tone techniques in modified form and in varied amounts, postromantic, neoclassic and neobaroque composers, pan-diatonicists and postimpressionists. Because we have no distinct "school" here and because the American composers shun an outright alliance with any one composer's ideas, we are still in the process of finding ourselves and, like Copland, our composers have "periods," not like the classic composers but in a peculiar manner of their own, wherein they adhere for a period to one concept such as romanticism, then enter a neoclassic phase, pass into a 12-tone period, and begin the attempt finally of settling on some synthesis of these varied elements. Attempts to place a label on them finds the labeler in a quandary since any one label fits only one series or even one piece alone of the composer's repertoire.

For an American author, there is a temptation to name and label a number approaching one hundred of the American contemporaries. The fact is that we have no way of knowing, at this point in history, whose music will persevere. If most of these composers are omitted, it is not a judgment of their worth, but rather limitations of space and a recognition of the small amount of keyboard interest on the composer's part.

AN EARLY INDEPENDENT COMPOSER

Charles Ives

America's first outstanding composer was so unique that he never founded a school nor indeed was discovered until he was aged. He is Charles Ives (1874-1954). His talent was so individual that he absorbed the techniques and knowledges of his teachers and then proceeded to use them in ways never dreamed of by his mentors. His curiosity and originality led him into a wide variety of musical experiments. He used bitonality probably quite independently of European composers and it is doubtful whether he was concerned with their efforts. He wrote three piano sonatas, and short pieces, often humorous. Since he was never concerned whether he received performances, it is not surprising to discover that his first sonata is long enough to constitute an entire program. His second sonata, while still very long, is almost feasible in the program sense though it is seldom performed in its entirety. This is entitled the *Concord Sonata*. His third sonata hardly deserves the name and he entitled it *Three Page Sonata*.

Ives drew musically from other sources besides his own imagination. One was the religious hymn or gospel song, the folk tunes and marches played by village bands which provided him with a varied fund of material. Another source was extramusical. Since he was a New Englander, he was widely read in the Transcendentalists headed by Emerson. He read Hawthorne and Thoreau and felt an affinity with this richly intellectual, poetic and spiritual group. In the famous *Concord Sonata* he adds one more influence. It is the striking opening motive of Beethoven's 5th Symphony, metamorphosed in ways never intended by Beethoven, to provide a unifying thread. The four movements are subtitled Emerson, Hawthorne, The Alcotts (at whose home the poetic group gathered), and Thoreau. In this sonata, Ives runs a gamut from the Beethoven theme, through Wagner's Wedding March, other marches, the song Loch Lomond, gospel tunes, and then the technical usages of polyrhythm, polytonality, harmonics, metre changes, and he even dispenses with metre. The work is monumental and it is a pity, in view of its many merits and beauties, to have to refer to its inadequacies in the shape of trite and banal sections and passages of crude and almost vulgar weakness. Ives broke with tutors and public alike (he was a successful insurance broker); he never subjected his compositions to performance and attendant criticism. The result was sadly uneven work which might have been refined to a point he never reached.

IMPRESSIONISM IN AMERICA

Charles Tomlinson Griffes

Charles Tomlinson Griffes (1884-1920) heads the list of minor American composers who based their work on the French Impressionist school. In his short life he wrote three sets of pieces which exemplify the amorphous side of impressionism. The best of these are the four popular pieces entitled *Four Roman Sketches*, Op. 7. They are subtitled *The White Peacock, The Fountain of The Acqua Paola, Nightfall,* and *Clouds.* The first two are the most frequently played. Griffes was sensitive and imaginative, but pitifully limited in the scope of his harmonic color and figuration compared to Debussy or Ravel. Of far greater worth is his Sonata in which he all but negates his atmospheric penchant and plunges into a forcefully dramatic and virtuosic display somewhat in the manner of Scriabin. If he had lived, he might indeed have developed into a major composer, in the light of this last intense offering, with its strong harmonic progressions, powerful dissonances, and terse rhythmic motives.

AMERICAN INDEPENDENCE

Aaron Copland

After this, the greatest American composers showed less interest in piano offerings. Aaron Copland (born 1900) is considered at this time to be the dean of truly American composition. His three periods have produced all too few piano works. During his study period with the famous composer-teacher, Nadia Boulanger, he wrote *The Cat And The Mouse,* a light, almost trivial scherzo. Then he produced a *Passacaglia,* a neoclassic, modal and somewhat dissonant piece of considerable power. In his later and still more classical period, he wrote one of the finest pieces of this century, a set of Variations, terse, brilliantly contrapuntal, highly dissonant, and powerful in their mounting intensity. Finally, he took a "second look" at 12-tone technique after an earlier rejection of this Schönbergian creation and wrote a discursive Fantasy. It is not wholly successful despite his great national reputation and it is doubtful whether it will live for posterity in the way the Variations will. One other composition, his Sonata, should be briefly discussed. It is a three movement work, the first movement is majestic, the second scherzando, and the third slow. Though it contains effective writing employing his skilled use, among other things, of metre changes (metrical transformation of rhythmic motives), dissonant counterpoint and register expansion, it is limited in its appeal and only occasionally performed.

Samuel Barber

Samuel Barber (born 1910) has written a set of Excursions, relatively superficial pieces employing jazz idioms, cowboy and mountain folk song and dance adaptations. His important keyboard work is a sonata which has become a representative American work in pianists' repertoire. It is in four movements, highly dissonant, employing, very dramatically, 12-tone devices at times (second theme of the first movement and the ostinato bass of the third movement), baroque contrapuntal devices (as in the fourth movement fugue), jazz elements (in the fugue) and brilliantly light scherzo writing in a kind of neo-Mendelssohnian style (second movement). It is difficult to classify the work, which might be called neoclassic, if it were not for the fervent emotionalism of the first movement, quite expressionistic in its intensity. Finally, he has written a *Nocturne*, a piece evocative of Fauré and Chopin, small but lovely.

Elliott Carter

Elliott Carter (born 1908) has written only one solo piano work, a very great Sonata (1946). His rhythmic preoccupation has resulted in an adaptation of an East Indian device called assymetric rhythm, used by various western composers including Stravinsky. A rapid small-valued unit such as a sixteenth note is preserved throughout a section of a piece in unvarying tempo but the number of these small units in larger groupings is constantly varied. In the classic period, the group of four-sixteenths was stable and reiterated. In Carter's writing, a group of four-sixteenths might be followed by three-sixteenths, which might in its turn be followed by seven-sixteenths, etc. This results in constantly irregular pulsation, disconcerting when first heard, but after becoming accustomed to this patterned irregularity, one finds the older-styled calm repetition static in comparison. This grand sonata shows considerable Copland influence, particularly in the slow movement, with plangent tonal chords in pan-diatonic progression. It is difficult to define the number of movements since the slow second movement dissolves into a very large, vibrantly rapid fugue, and then returns to a transposition of the slow movement. If it were not for this return, fixing the overall structure (from the beginning of the second movement) as an ABA, it might have been considered as two distinct movements. As a consequence of this return, however, it must be called one very large movement, making the entire sonata a two movement form. It is a magnificent work, exhibiting a fine intellectuality, allied with intense emotion and impeccable taste. It is a pity that its technical difficulty discourages its study since it deservedly occupies a position as one of the truly great piano works of this century. Carter has also written a piano concerto, of such polyrhythmic intricacy that it will be remarkable if it receives any but the most infrequent performance. This is also true, if somewhat less so, of many of this century's large keyboard works, with relatively few pianists willing to devote the many months of study required for their adequate preparation.

Roger Sessions

A composer who has influenced many Americans, both as teacher and colleague, is Roger Sessions (born 1896). He has written two power- ful sonatas, a set of smaller pieces, *From My Diary,* and some pieces for children. His style is propellant, motoric, vitally dissonant. He shuns tonality and uses a complicated chromaticism and rhythmic intricacy. A necessary prerequisite to a proper understanding of the two larger works is a familiarity with the short four pieces from the *Diary.* One of these is embryonic in its relationship to the sonatas, a fast-slow-fast piece easily grasped and a miniature of what the larger works proclaim.

Vincent Persichetti

Vincent Persichetti (born 1915) is a fine, prolific composer for the piano with ten sonatas, six sonatinas, two volumes of *Poems* (character pieces) and children's music. His writing is highly varied, employing tonal and non-tonal elements, bitonality, contrapuntal devices, and homo- phony. He also uses literary allusions such as lines of contemporary poetry for titles and subtitles. His work has a post-romantic subjective quality, intensely lyrical, and while none of his pieces display the dra- matic intensity of a Barber or Carter, he writes well enough to enjoy the admiration and performance of many musicians. His Sonatinas and Poems are felicitous study pieces for young pianists whose teachers feel a debt of gratitude to the composer.

Norman Dello Joio

Norman Dello Joio (born 1913) has written several sonatas contain- ing some harmonic variety but usually revealing pan-diatonic homophony or tonal-type counterpoint. The music is not sufficiently intense nor varied enough to bring pianists to their enthusiastic performance though the sonatas are quite easy to learn and memorize in comparison with much contemporary music.

Henry Cowell

Henry Cowell (1897-1965) deserves mention for his earnest if not very successful search for ways to enlarge pianistic possibilities. He has advocated the use of the entire forearm pressed into the key- board for "tone clusters," has asked the pianist to reach into the body of the instrument and pluck strings, has required direct hand sliding within the piano for a type of glissando and sliding fingers along the length of the strings to produce an eerie "banshee" wail. Much of his piano music was written to exploit these effects but it has never been taken seriously, nor has his effect-free music shown outstanding talent.

John Cage

John Cage (born 1912) has gone several steps beyond Cowell and has "prepared" a piano in order to drastically alter its timbres by placing objects within the body of the instrument at various spots on the sound board or attached to the strings. This preparation usually requires several hours and renders the doubtful result impractical. He has also created a kind of notation much more akin to a scientific graph than the traditional notation and enlisted a small select group of followers in his experiments. While it is dangerous to predict, very little of his accomplishment will probably have an enduring value.

Alan Hovaness

Alan Hovaness (born 1911), though American born, makes as much of his Armenian ancestry in music as any native Armenian. His output is voluminous, eastern in quality, with a peculiarly static or moveless feeling. He uses harmonies and scales from his ancestral past, toys with simple rhythm accent displacements, and has achieved a measure of popularity, especially as his piano works are not difficult to play. He has sonatas, sonatinas, dances, and character pieces.

This incomplete listing of American piano composers neglects many, names like Arthur Berger, Halsey Stevens, Ross Lee Finney, William Bergsma, Paul Bowles, and so on. However, just as one must start somewhere, so one must stop before the list assumes encyclopedic proportions The difficulty, not only of assessing enduring value in a contemporary, but of deciding whom to omit, is sufficiently great to cause any compiler to be somewhat haunted by a sense of inadequacy. The development of piano music in the United States leaves some conflict of feeling in the pianist-musician's mind. The volume, while great, is mainly so because of the number of composers, but disappointing in the paucity of the individual production. Perhaps it is too much to expect the twentieth-century composer to (a) like the piano as much as the nineteenth-century composer, or (b) write on the voluminous scale that nineteenth-century composers did. The twentieth-century composer starts his piano composing career with far more fixed ideas on the keyboard sound than did his predecessors and, with few exceptions, does not depart from the limited frame into which he has set the keyboard.

THE NON-AMERICANS

Ernst Křenek

It is difficult to know how to classify those non-American (by birth) composers who have spent so many years here that they defy classification in other countries. Ernst Křenek (born 1900) is a transplanted Austrian composer who has lived, taught, and composed for many years in the United States. An ardent follower of Schönberg, he finally settled on an exclusive adherence to the 12-tone system. His smaller pieces are admirably instructive and are embodied in two opuses, Twelve Short Piano Pieces, Op. 83, and Eight Piano Pieces issued some eight years later. But the main body of his piano creation is contained in his six sonatas, some sonatinas and suites as well as variations and miscellaneous short works. His style, within the framework he has assumed, is highly varied, very pianistic (fitting well in the hands of the pianist) and with intense expression.

Ernst Toch

Ernst Toch (born 1887) is another Austrian who has been in the United States for many years. He has developed his style from a pure nineteenth-century romantically tonal character piece type of writing to a much more severe contrapuntal and chromatic linear style. He has written many pieces, études, and character types. His *Juggler* still remains a student favorite for its sprightliness and wrist exercise.

LATIN AMERICA: INFLUENCES

The history of keyboard music in South and Central America is abbreviated by its cultural history which traditionally derives so much from the European countries from whence came its progenitors. The Spaniards and Portuguese who settled an entire continent brought a limited supply of their cultural homeland with them. As the countries developed, more was fed into them from Europe, until finally the young artists of all fields began to return to the fountainheads and discovered that other countries, France, Germany, and Italy, had much to offer to their taste. Embedded in their musical heritage were the rhythms, the scales, dances, and tunes of their ancestral homes. These they had begun to combine, at long last and to only a small degree, with the native Indian rhythmic elements. In addition, on their European study pilgrimages, they found French and German elements to use as leavening, especially as the nineteenth century saw an increasing number of non-Iberian Europeans emigrating to South America, especially German and Italian.

Music in South America has been greatly increased in the last seventy-five years. The composers, by and large, have been of the romantic-nationalist persuasion. Now there is a growing international body, still too young, however, to have made a significant contribution to the great bulk of western music. Therefore, the composers, few in number, cited here, are mainly nationalists, or better regionalists, basing their concepts on their homeland's native offerings.

COMPOSERS

Heitor Villa-Lobos

Chief among these is Heitor Villa-Lobos (1887-1959) of Brazil. Practically self-taught except for a period of study in France, he reminds one of Charles Ives in North America, because he exhibits the weaknesses as well as strengths of uncriticized and hence undisciplined work. He assimilated the folk element of his Portuguese ancestry and plunged into the jungle to seek out Indian rhythm and tune sources. His very large repertoire varies from almost pure impressionism through simple folk song settings to the most highly organized rhythm combinations and even neoclassical adaptations. His *Baby's Family* pieces combine folk tunes with attractively dissonant virtuosity as in the *Polichinelle*. His *Three Maries* do much the same as also do his *Practical Guides*, several volumes of piano pieces of graduated difficulty. His later *Bachianas Brasileiras*, a whimsical treatment combining folk and Bach elements in several pieces, contain four piano examples. His most popular piece is the Choros No. 5, *The Soul of Brazil*. It is in several short sections with a reprise, beginning languorously with a slow rhythmically reiterated background motive and a far-spaced rhapsodic theme, repeated with a cross-rhythmed additional voice, changing into a lilting cantina-like melody, and abruptly clangorous with rough, dissonant harmonies, savagely Indian rhythms and polyrhythmic counterpoint, finally subsiding into its opening theme and mood.

His largest-scaled effort for the keyboard is his *Rudepôema*, written for the great pianist, Arthur Rubinstein, who was instrumental in the promotion of his unusual talent. The piece, however, is overlong, discursive, and poorly structured and, as a result, is never played. It has large virtuosic passages and many separated areas of musical worth, separated by areas not so worthy. This last criticism is frequently voiced about Villa-Lobos and reference has already been made to the juxtaposition of beauty and banality in his compositions.

Alberto Ginastera

Of equal worth and far more solidly grounded is Alberto Ginastera of Argentina (born 1916). He has explored and assimilated his native folk music almost as completely as Villa-Lobos, but is far more eclectic in his usage of styles. Blessed with a superior intellectual quality which in no way detracts from his driving, motoric penchant, he has written many kinds of music, *Argentinian Dances,* and other nationalist dance and folk song settings, a set of Twelve American Preludes, dedicated to and evocative of various composers of both Americas, and a large dramatic sonata with marked metric and rhythmic schemes, extensive virtuosity, dramatic, mysterious, improvisatory, and declamatory. His harmony is harshly bold. His influence is greatly felt on both continents and it is a certainty that he will be considered one of this century's outstanding composers.

VARIOUS COMPOSERS

There are many more composers who shall have to suffer brief mention. In Chile, Humberto Allende (born 1885) has written charming if somewhat dated pieces, as Tonadas (tunes) or as Etudes. They are pleasant pieces, not profound, unpretentious but exhibiting good taste. His much younger compatriot, Juan Orriego Salas (born 1919) has still to prove his mature style. He has studied in the United States and his piano music, two suites, Variations And Fugue, are all that is available at present. Juan José Castro (born 1895) of Argentina writes pleasantly also, though not profoundly, in a Toccata and Spanish Sonatina. Camargo Guarnieri of Brazil (born 1907) delights in dance rhythms as evidenced by his Brazilian Dance based on the popular Samba, but he also writes exceedingly difficult virtuosic pieces as shown in his chromatic and double-noted Toccata. He also has three volumes of Preludes, sonatinas, and other pieces.

Carlos Chavez

Perhaps the third in importance of the southland's outstanding composers after Villa-Lobos and Ginastera is Carlos Chavez (born 1899). He has been dubbed the father of Mexican music and his large number of musical progeny in the form of pupils bears out his title. Like all his contemporaries, he has first based his work on the folk heritage of his country and made it a prime ingredient of his total expression. The result, when this is blended with his imagination and other contemporary elements, is a harshly dissonant but authentic expression of a powerful personality. He has written sonatas, preludes, and various short pieces in which he exploits both dance rhythms and abstract patterns. He remains a controversial figure as many deem his music too uncompromising to be a true artistic expression unrelieved by lyrical elements and too often over-percussive.

Juan Carlos Paz

In 1930, a group formed in Argentina, calling themselves The Renovators, a league to bring South American music up to date by the introduction and usage of the contemporary idioms. Juan Carlos Paz (born 1897) is a distinguished founder who has run the gamut from romanticism through neoclassicism to 12-tone expressionism in many piano pieces including a Sonatina, Ten Tone-Row Pieces, Songs And Ballades, and many earlier works.

Francisco Mignone

Francisco Mignone of Brazil (born 1897) has written voluminously for piano. Of Italian ancestry, he has plumbed Brazilian folk music and used it in his writing though he has no gift to compare with Villa-Lobos. He has written a sonata and sonatinas, waltzes, and national-type ballads and studies.

This brings to a close a far too brief glimpse of the South American piano compositional scene. It is not calculated to do justice to a teeming continent coming awake musically, nor is it meant as more than a glimpse. As in so many other areas of musical activity, far more is produced than can be noted and we can only hope that the verdict of history will be more just and considered than is possible here.

SUGGESTED READING

Chase, G. *America's Music*. New York: McGraw-Hill Book Company, 1955, pp. 302-323 (Gottschalk); pp. 345-364 (MacDowell); pp. 493-501 (Copland); pp. 517-520 (Griffes); pp. 525-530 (Sessions); pp. 664-678 (Ives).

Cowell, H. *Charles Ives and His Music*. New York: Oxford University Press, 1955, pp. 190-203 (Concord Sonata).

Gillespie, J. *Five Centuries of Keyboard Music*. Belmont, Calif.: Wadsworth Publishing Co., Inc., 1965, pp. 393-405 (Latin American Composers); pp. 407-425 (U.S. Composers).

Hansen, P. S. *An Introduction to 20th-Century Music*. Boston: Allyn & Bacon, Inc., 1961, pp. 81-88 (Ives); pp. 321-329 (Copland).

Howard, J. T. *Our American Music.* New York: Crowell, 1931, pp. 378-403
(MacDowell); pp. 209-215 (Gottschalk); pp. 485-487 (Griffes).
Ives, C. *Essays Before a Sonata and Other Writings.* New York: W. W. Nor-
ton & Company, Inc., 1962, pp. 11-69 (The Concord Sonata).
Kirby, F. E. *A Short History of Keyboard Music.* New York: The Free
Press, 1966, pp. 444-458 (North and South American Composers).
Machlis, J. *Introduction to Contemporary Music.* New York: W. W. Norton
& Company, Inc., 1961, pp. 454, 455 (Griffes); pp. 481-484 (Copland).
Slonimsky, N. *Music in Latin America.* New York: Crowell, 1945, pp. 72-81
(Argentinian music sources); pp. 109-123 (Brazilian sources); pp. 142-
150 (Villa-Lobos); pp. 214-225 (Mexican sources); pp. 230-235 (Chavez).

SUGGESTED WRITTEN ASSIGNMENTS

1. Who was the first "American" composer and why was he so designated?
2. Why cannot MacDowell be considered a representative American composer?
3. What happens to twentieth-century American composers because of their
   lack of adherence to a "school"?
4. Can you give a reason for the uneven quality in the works of Charles
   Ives?
5. What were the extramusical influences as well as the musical ones on
   Charles Ives?
6. From what influence was Griffes emerging at the end of his life and
   which composition showed this change?
7. What periods are represented in the music of Aaron Copland?
8. What piece by Copland bears the stamp of greatness?
9. What do Barber and Carter have in common in a large-scaled work?
10. Name the three most prominent composers south of our border.
11. What is the predominating influence in South and Central American
    music?

SUGGESTED LISTENING

1. GOTTSCHALK—*March of the Gibaros*
2. GRIFFES—Piano Sonata
3. REINAGLE—Sonata in E Major
4. KŘENEK—*Bagatelles* (4 hands)
5. IVES—Sonata No. 2 (Concord)
6. VILLA-LOBOS—*Alma Brasileira*

SUGGESTED ADDITIONAL LISTENING

1. MACDOWELL—Sonata No. 4 (Keltic)
2. COPLAND—Variations
3. BARBER—Sonata
4. CARTER—Sonata
5. SESSIONS—Sonata No. 1
6. DELLO JOIO—Sonata No. 3
7. CAGE—Sonatas and Interludes for Prepared Piano

8. COWELL—Piano Music
9. GINASTERA—Sonata (1952)
10. CASTRO—*Sonatina Española*
11. CHAVEZ—Poligonos and Unidad
12. GRIFFES—Roman Sketches, Op. 7
13. COPLAND—Piano Fantasy (1957)
14. COPLAND—Piano Sonata (1941)
15. VILLA-LOBOS—Prole do Bebe (Suites Nos. 1 and 2)

Discography

Extensive use has been made of record collections, particularly for the early music of the Baroque era. RCA Victor's *History of Music in Sound;* Decca's (DEC) DL8019 *Harpsichord Music;* Experiences Anonymes (EA) *English Keyboard Music;* Haydn Society's (HS) *Masterpieces of Music;* Vanguard's (VAN) *Masterpieces of the Italian Baroque;* L'Oiseau Lyre's (OIS) *Clavichord Recordings* and *Archive Recordings* (ARC) have been those most used or consulted. Many music department libraries contain these well-known collections, rendering it practical for the student to hear selections included in the suggested listening. In addition to the above labels, the remainder of the recordings listed are to be found in the Schwan catalogue.

The following is a repetition of the suggested listening by chapters for the convenience of student and instructor:

Chapter 1
1. BACH—The Two-Part Inventions
2. FROBERGER—*Lamentation for Ferdinand IV*
3. FRESCOBALDI—*Toccata d'Intavolatura*
4. CHOPIN—Etudes, Op. 10, Nos. 4 and 5
5. DEBUSSY—Prélude *The Sunken Cathedral*

Chapter 2
1. BULL—In Nomine
2. BULL—My Selfe
3. TOMKINS—*Fortune My Foe*
4. GIBBON—The King's Juell
5. BYRD—The Earl of Salisbury
6. BYRD—The Bells

7. Anonymous—*Oh, ye Happy Dames* (EA, Eng. Key. Ma.)
8. Farnaby—*Loth to Depart*
9. Edwards—*When Griping Griefs*
10. Byrd—*Ut, Re, Mi, Fa, Sol, La*
11. Purcell—*A New Ground* (Variations)
12. Anonymous—*Galliard* (EA, see above)
13. Anonymous—*My Lady Carey's Dompe* (RCA, Vol. 4)
14. Purcell—Suites
15. Peerson—*The Fall of the Leafe*
16. Farnaby—*A Toye*
17. Munday—*Tres Partes In Una*
18. Purcell—*Hornpipe*

Chapter 3
1. Frescobaldi—*Capriccio sopra un Soggetto*
2. Frescobaldi—*Three Galliards*
3. D. Scarlatti—Sonata in B♭ (Longo 498)
4. A. Scarlatti—Toccatas
5. B. Pasquini—Canzona
6. Zipoli—Harpsichord Suites
7. Galuppi—Sonatas (4 and 5)
8. Platti—Sonata No. 1 in D
9. Grazioli—Sonata in B♭
10. D. Scarlatti—Sonatas (Longo 385, 387)
11. Rutini—Andante
12. Martini—Allegro
13. Matielli—Adagio
14. Frescobaldi—Four Correnti
15. Frescobaldi—*Canzone primo, seconda, quarta*
16. Frescobaldi—Partite Sopra L'Aria de Ruggiero

Chapter 4
1. Chambonnières—*Sarabande, Drollerie, Allemande dit L'Affligée, Volte*
2. Lully—Courante
3. Loeillet—Gigue from G Minor Suite
4. L. Couperin—Chaconne in D Minor
5. F. Couperin—*Rigaudon en Rondeau* (Vendangeuses)
6. F. Couperin—8th Ordre
7. F. Couperin—*La Favorite*
8. L. Couperin—*Branle de Basque, Pavanne, Pasacaille*
9. Rameau—*Les Cyclops*
10. Rameau—*Le Rappel des Oiseaux*
11. Rameau—Suite, A Minor
12. Zweelinck—Variations on *My Young Life Has to End*
13. Cabezón—*Diferencias Sobre "La Gallarda Milanesa"*
14. Cabanilles—*Tiento de Falsas*
15. Soler—Sonatas
16. Nebra—Sonata

Chapter 5
1. FROBERGER—Suite No. 14, G Minor (Clavichord)
2. KUHNAU—Biblical Sonatas
3. TELEMANN—Fantasias
4. J. S. BACH—*Chromatic Fantasy; Capriccio on the Departure of a Beloved Brother; Partita No. 2, C Minor*
5. C.P.E. BACH—Prussian Sonata in A
6. J. C. BACH—Sonatas
7. FROBERGER—*Tombeau de M. Blanchroche;* Fantasia, Ricercar
8. HANDEL—Suites (esp. D Minor)
9. BÖHM—Suites
10. BUXTEHUDE—Capricciosa
11. FISCHER—*Passacaglia* and *Passepied*
12. KRIEGER—Suite
13. W. F. BACH—Fantasia and Fugue
14. J. S. BACH—Toccata in E Minor

Chapter 6
1. HAYDN—Sonata in E♭, No. 52
2. HAYDN—Variations in F Minor
3. MOZART—Variations on *Ah, vous dirai je, Maman*
4. MOZART—Sonata in C Major, K. 330
5. MOZART—Fantasia in C Minor, K. 475
6. BEETHOVEN—Sonata, Op. 2 No. 2
7. BEETHOVEN—Sonata, Op. 109
8. BEETHOVEN—32 Variations in C Minor
9. HAYDN—Sonata No. 34, E Minor
10. HAYDN—Fantasy in D Major
11. HAYDN—Sonata No. 50 in C Major
12. MOZART—Variations on *Salve Tu, Domine*
13. MOZART—Fantasia in C Minor, K. 396
14. MOZART—Sonata in A Minor, K. 310
15. MOZART—Sonata in B♭ Major, K. 333
16. BEETHOVEN—The Diabelli Variations
17. BEETHOVEN—Bagatelles, Op. 119 and Op. 126
18. BEETHOVEN—Sonata, Op. 81A *Les Adieux*
19. BEETHOVEN—Concerto No. 4 for Piano and Orchestra in G Major

Chapter 7
1. WEBER—Sonata in E Minor
2. SCHUBERT—*Impromptus,* Op. 90
3. SCHUBERT—Sonata in A, Op. 120
4. MENDELSSOHN—Serious Variations
5. SCHUMANN—Symphonic Études
6. BRAHMS—Variations on a Theme by Handel
7. BRAHMS—Piano Pieces, Op. 76
8. LISZT—*Transcendental Études Mazeppa* and *Feux Follets*
9. CHOPIN—Études Op. 10

10. WEBER—Invitation to the Dance
11. SCHUBERT—Sonata B♭ Major (posthumous)
12. SCHUBERT—*Wanderer Fantasy*
13. SCHUBERT—*Moments Musicaux*, Op. 94
14. MENDELSSOHN—Hunting Song and Spinning Song from Songs Without Words
15. SCHUMANN—*Fantasia*, Op. 17
16. SCHUMANN—Carnaval
17. BRAHMS—Sonata in F Minor, Op. 5
18. BRAHMS—Scherzo, E♭ Minor, Op. 4
19. BRAHMS—Rhapsody in E♭, Op. 119
20. LISZT—Hungarian Rhapsodies, Nos. 2, 6, 12
21. LISZT—Paganini Étude *La Campanella*
22. LISZT—Petrarch Sonnet No. 104
23. CHOPIN—*Barcarolle*
24. CHOPIN—Scherzo, B-flat Minor, Op. 31
25. CHOPIN—Fantasy, Op. 49

Chapter 8

1. MUSSORGSKY—*Pictures from an Exhibition*
2. SCRIABIN—Préludes, Op. 11
3. RACHMANINOFF—*Tableaux Études*, Op. 33
4. PROKOFIEFF—Sonata No. 3
5. SHOSTAKOVICH—Sonata No. 2
6. KABALEVSKY—Sonata No. 3
7. SCRIABIN—Sonata No. 5 *Poem of Ecstasy*
8. RACHMANINOFF—Prelude, G♯ Minor, Op. 23 No. 12; Prelude, G Major, Op. 23 No. 6
9. PROKOFIEFF—Suggestion Diabolique
10. PROKOFIEFF—Toccata, Op. 11
11. PROKOFIEFF—Sonata No. 6
12. SHOSTAKOVICH—Prélude and Fugue, D♭, Op. 87
13. SHOSTAKOVICH—Three Fantastic Dances
14. KABALEVSKY—Children's Pieces, Op. 27
15. KABALEVSKY—Sonatine, Op. 13
16. MEDTNER—*Fairy Tales*, Op. 20
17. BALAKIREV—*Islamey*

Chapter 9

1. FRANCK—Prélude, Chorale and Fugue
2. SAINT-SAËNS—Piano Music
3. FAURÉ—Nocturne No. 2, B Major
4. DEBUSSY—Prélude *The Interrupted Serenade;* Prelude *Fireworks*
5. RAVEL—*Gaspard de la Nuit*
6. POULENC—*Improvisations*
7. MILHAUD—*The Seven-Branched Candelabra*
8. MESSIAEN—Nine Meditations
9. FRANÇAIS—Concertino for Piano and Orchestra
10. HONEGGER—Concertino for Piano and Orchestra

11. FRANCK—Symphonic Variations for Piano and Orchestra
12. FAURÉ—Barcarolle, Op. 66, F♯ Minor; Theme and Variations, Op. 73
13. POULENC—Toccata; *Les Soirées de Nazelles*
14. RAVEL—*Le Tombeau de Couperin; Miroirs*
15. DEBUSSY—*Isle Joyeuse; Poissons d'or; Reflets dans l'Eau*

Chapter 10
1. BARTÓK—Suite for Piano, Op. 14
2. SZYMANOWSKI—Mazurkas, Op. 50
3. GRIEG—Lyric Pieces, Op. 12, Op. 38, Op. 43
4. NIELSEN—Suite, Op. 45
5. NIELSEN—Symphonic Suite, Op. 8; 3 Piano Pieces, Op. 59
6. BARTÓK—Sonatina for Piano; Sonata for Piano (1926); Rhapsody, Op. 1; Out of Doors; Sonata for 2 Pianos and Percussion; Mikrokosmos Vol. 6; *Improvisations*, Op. 20
7. BUSONI—Fantasia Contrappuntistica (2 pianos); Piano Transcriptions of Bach Chorale Preludes
8. KODÁLY—9 Pieces for Piano (1910); 7 Pieces for Piano, Op. 11
9. BAX—Mediterranean (1921)
10. TCHEREPNIN—Concerto No. 2 for Piano and Orchestra
11. GRIEG—Sonata, Op. 7, E Minor

Chapter 11
1. ALBÉNIZ—*Triana* from *Iberia*
2. GRANADOS—Maiden and the Nightingale from *Goyescas*
3. DE FALLA—4 Pièces *Espagnoles*
4. TURINA—*Sevilla* Suite
5. ALBÉNIZ—*Evocacion* from *Iberia; Navarra; El Puerto* from *Iberia*
6. GRANADOS—*Danzas Españolas* (1900); *Los Requiebros* from *Goyescas; El Fandango del Candil* from *Goyescas*
7. DE FALLA—*Fantasia Baetica;* Ritual Fire Dance
8. TURINA—*Contes d'Espagne*
9. MOMPOU—*Impresiones Intimas*
10. ESPLA—*Sonata Española*, Op. 53
11. RODRIGO, J.—*Danzas de España*

Chapter 12
1. HINDEMITH—Sonata No. 3 (1936)
2. SCHÖNBERG—Three Piano Pieces, Op. 11
3. STOCKHAUSEN—11 Piano Pieces (1954-61)
4. BERG—Sonata, Op. 1
5. WEBERN—Variations
6. SCHÖNBERG—Suite for Piano, Op. 25; Five Piano Pieces, Op. 23
7. HINDEMITH—Suite 1922, Op. 26

Chap. 13
1. GOTTSCHALK—*March of the Gibaros*
2. GRIFFES—Piano Sonata
3. REINAGLE—Sonata in E Major

4. KŘENEK—*Bagatelles* (4 hands)
5. IVES—Sonata No. 2 (Concord)
6. VILLA-LOBOS—*Alma Brasileira*
7. MACDOWELL—Sonata No. 4 (Keltic)
8. COPLAND—Variations
9. BARBER—Sonata
10. CARTER—Sonata
11. SESSIONS—Sonata No. 1
12. DELLO JOIO—Sonata No. 3
13. CAGE—Sonatas and Interludes for Prepared Piano
14. COWELL—Piano Music
15. GINASTERA—Sonata (1952)
16. CASTRO—*Sonatina Española*
17. CHAVEZ—Poligonos and Unidad
18. GRIFFES—Roman Sketches, Op. 7
19. COPLAND—Piano Fantasy (1957); Piano Sonata (1941)
20. VILLA-LOBOS—Prole do Bebe (Suites Nos. 1 and 2)

Bibliography

GENERAL BIBLIOGRAPHY

APEL, WILLI, *Harvard Dictionary of Music*, Cambridge: Harvard University Press, 1944.

APEL, WILLI, *Masters of the Keyboard*, Cambridge: Harvard University Press, 1947.

BACH, C. P. E., *Essay on the True Art of Playing Keyboard Instruments*, (trans. by W. Mitchell), New York: W. W. Norton & Company, Inc., 1949.

BAUER, M., *Twentieth Century Music*, New York: G. P. Putnam & Sons, 1947.

BLOM, E., (Editor) *Grove's Dictionary of Music and Musicians*, 5th edition, London: Macmillan & Co., Ltd., 1954.

BLOM, E., *The Romance of the Piano*, London: Foulis, 1928.

BUKOFZER, M., *Music in the Baroque Era*, New York: W. W. Norton & Company, Inc., 1947.

COLLAER, P. *A History of Modern Music*, (trans. by S. Abeles) New York: Grosset & Dunlap, Inc., 1961.

DALE, K., *Nineteenth Century Piano Music*, London: Oxford University Press, 1954.

DANNREUTHER, E., *Musical Ornamentation*, London: Novello and Co., Ltd., 1893.

DART, T., *The Interpretation of Music*, London: Hutchinson's Universal Library, 1954.

DAVISON, A. and APEL, W., *Historical Anthology of Music*, Harvard University Press, 2 vol., 1946, 1950.

DEMUTH, N., *French Piano Music*, Museum Press Ltd., no date.

DOLMETSCH, A., *The Interpretation of the Music of the XVII and XVIII Centuries*, London: Novello and Co., Ltd., 1946.

EINSTEIN, A., *Music in the Romantic Era*, New York: W. W. Norton & Company, Inc., 1947.

FERGUSON, D., *The Piano Music of Six Great Composers*, New York: Prentice-Hall, Inc., 1947.

FRISKIN, J. and FREUNDLICH, I., *Music for the Piano*, New York: Holt, Rinehart & Winston, Inc., 1954.

GILLESPIE, J., *Five Centuries of Keyboard Music,* Belmont, California: Wadsworth Publishing Co., 1965.

GROUT, D. J., *A History of Western Music,* New York: W. W. Norton & Company, Inc., 1960.

HAMILTON, C. G., *Piano Music,* Boston: Oliver Ditson Co., 1925.

HANSEN, P. S., *An Introduction to Twentieth Century Music,* Boston: Allyn & Bacon, Inc., 1961.

HUTCHESON, E., *The Literature of the Piano,* 2nd ed., New York: Alfred A. Knopf, Inc., 1949.

JEAN-AUBRY, G., *An Introduction to French Music,* London: Palmer and Hayward, 1917.

KENYON, M., *Harpsichord Music,* London, Cassell and Company, Ltd., 1949.

KIRBY, F. E., *A Short History of Keyboard Music,* New York: The Free Press, 1966.

LANDOWSKA, W., *Music of the Past,* (trans. by W. A. Bradley), New York: Alfred A. Knopf, Inc., 1924.

LANG, P. H., *Music in Western Civilization,* New York: W. W. Norton & Company, Inc., 1941.

LEONARD, R. A., *A History of Russian Music,* New York: The Macmillan Co., 1957.

LOCKWOOD, A., *Notes on the Literature of the Piano,* Ann Arbor: University of Michigan Press, 1940.

LOESSER, A., *Men, Women and Pianos,* New York: Simon & Schuster, Inc., 1954.

MACHLIS, J., *Introduction to Contemporary Music,* New York, W. W. Norton & Company, Inc., 1961.

NEWMAN, W. S., *The Sonata in the Baroque Era,* Chapel Hill: The University of North Carolina Press, 1959.

NEWMAN, W. S., *The Sonata in the Classic Era,* Chapel Hill: The University of North Carolina Press, 1963.

SCHOLES, P. A., (Editor) *The Oxford Companion to Music,* 9th edition, London: Oxford University Press, 1955.

SHEDLOCK, J. S., *The Pianoforte Sonata,* London: Methuen and Co., Ltd., 1895.

SLONIMSKY, N., *Music Since* 1900, New York: Coleman-Ross, 1949.

THOMPSON, O., (Editor) *The International Cyclopedia of Music and Musicians,* New York: Dodd, Mead & Co., 1939.

WEITZMANN, C. F., *A History of Pianoforte Playing* (trans. by T. Baker), New York: G. Schirmer, 1897.

WESTERBY, H., *The History of Pianoforte Music,* London: Kogan Paul, Trench, Trubner & Co., Ltd., 1924.

SECONDARY LITERATURE

BADURA-SKODA, E. and P., *Interpreting Mozart on the Keyboard,* New York: St. Martin's Press, 1962.

BERGER, A., *Aaron Copland,* New York: Oxford University Press, 1953.

BERTENSSON, S., and LEYDA J., *Sergei Rachmaninoff,* New York: New York University Press, 1956.

BODKY, E., *The Interpretation of Bach's Keyboard Works,* Cambridge, Mass.: Harvard University Press, 1960.

BORREN, C. von den, *The Sources of Keyboard Music in England* (trans. by J. Matthew), London: Novello and Co., Ltd., 1913.

BROWN, M. J. E., *Schubert*, New York: St. Martin's Press, 1958.

BURK, J. N., *Mozart and His Music*, New York: Random House, Inc., 1959.

BURK, J. N., *The Life and Works of Beethoven*, New York: Modern Library, 1946.

CALVOCORESSI, N. D. and ABRAHAM, G., *Masters of Russian Music*, New York: Alfred A. Knopf, Inc., 1936.

CHASE, G., *The Music of Spain*, New York: Dover Publications, Inc., 1959.

CHASE, G., *America's Music*, New York: McGraw-Hill Book Co., 1955.

CLOSSON, E., *The History of the Piano* (trans. by D. Ames), London: Paul Elek, 1947.

COPLAND, A., *Music and Imagination*, Cambridge, Mass.: Harvard University Press, 1952.

CORTOT, A., *In Search of Chopin* (trans. by C. and R. Clarke, New York: Abelard Press, 1952.

COWELL, H. and S., *Charles Ives and His Music*, New York: Oxford University Press, 1955.

DAVID, H. T. and MENDEL, A., *The Bach Reader*, New York: W. W. Norton & Company, Inc., 1945.

EINSTEIN, A., *Mozart, His Character, His Work*, New York: Oxford University Press, 1945.

EINSTEIN, A., *Schubert*, New York: Oxford University Press, 1951.

EMERY, W., *Bach's Ornaments*, London: Novello & Co., 1953.

FULLER-MAITLAND, J. A. and SQUIRE, W. B., *Introduction to the Fitzwilliam Virginal Book*, Leipzig: Breitkopf and Hartel, 1899.

GALPIN, F. W., *Old English Instruments of Music*, London: Methuen and Co., 1932.

GEIRINGER, K., *Brahms, His Life and Work*, New York: Oxford University Press, 1947.

GEIRINGER, K., *The Bach Family*, New York: Oxford University Press, 1954.

GEIRINGER, K., *Haydn*, New York: W. W. Norton & Company, Inc., 1946.

GLYN, M., *About Elizabethan Virginal Music and Its Composers*, London, 1924.

GOSS, M., *Bolero, The Life of Ravel*, Tudor, 1940.

HARICH-SCHNEIDER, E., *The Harpsichord*, Kassel, Barenreiter, 1954.

HIPKINS, A. J., *Musical Instruments*, London: A. & C. Black, Ltd., 1921.

HIPKINS, A. J., *The Pianoforte*, London: Novello, Ewer and Co., 1896.

HOWARD, J. T., *Our American Music*, New York: Thomas Y. Crowell Co., 1931.

HUBBARD, F., *Three Centuries of Harpsichord Making*, Cambridge, Mass.: Harvard University Press, 1965.

IVES, C., *Essays Before a Sonata and Other Writings*, New York: W. W. Norton & Company, Inc., 1962.

JACOB, H. E., *Felix Mendelssohn and His Times* (trans. by R. and C. Winston), Englewood Cliffs, New Jersey: Prentice-Hall, Inc., 1963.

JAMES, P., *Early Keyboard Instruments*, London: Peter Davies, Ltd., 1930.

JANKELEVITCH, V., *Ravel*, New York: Grove Press, Inc., 1959.

KIRKPATRICK, R., *Domenico Scarlatti*, Princeton: Princeton University Press, 1953.

LOCKSPEISER, E., *Debussy, His Life and Mind*, New York: The Macmillan Co., 1962.

MONTAGUE-NATHAN, M., *Contemporary Russian Composers,* London: Palmer and Hayward, 1917.

NAYLOR, E. W., *An Elizabethan Virginal Book,* New York: E. P. Dutton & Co., Inc., 1905.

NESTYEV, I. V., *Prokofiev,* Stanford: Stanford University Press, 1960.

NEUPERT, H., *Harpsichord Manual,* Kassel, Barenreiter, 1960.

NIECKS, F., *Robert Schumann,* London: J. M. Dent & Sons, Ltd., 1924.

NIEMANN, W., *Brahms,* (trans. by C. A. Phillips), New York: Grosset & Dunlap, Inc., 1946.

REESER, E., *The Sons of Bach,* Stockholm: Continental Book Co., 1946.

RIMBAULT, E. F., *The Pianoforte,* London: Robert Cocks and Co., 1860.

RUBIO, FATHER S., *Introduction to the Sonatas of Padre Soler,* Madrid: Union Musical Espanola, 1957.

SACHS, C., *World History of the Dance,* (trans. by B. Schonberg), New York: W. W. Norton & Company, Inc., 1937.

SALAZAR, A., *Music in Our Time,* New York: W. W. Norton & Company, Inc., 1946.

SCHMITZ, E. R., *The Piano Works of Claude Debussy,* New York: Duell, Sloan and Pearce, 1950.

SCHÖNBERG, A., *Style and Ideas,* New York: Philosophical Library, Inc., 1950.

SITWELL, S., *Liszt,* New York: Houghton Mifflin Co., 1934.

SLONIMSKY, N., *Music in Latin America,* New York: Thomas Y. Crowell Co., 1945.

SPITTA, P., *J. S. Bach,* New York: Dover Publications, Inc., 1951.

STEVENS, H., *The Life and Music of Bela Bartók,* New York: Oxford University Press, 1953.

THAYER, A. W., *The Life of Ludwig von Beethoven,* (ed. H. E. Krehbiel), New York: Beethoven Association, 1921.

THOMPSON, O., *Debussy, Man and Artist,* New York: Dodd, Mead & Co., 1937.

TOVEY, D., *The Forms of Music,* Cleveland: World Publishing Co., 1963.

WEINSTOCK, H., *Chopin, The Man and His Music,* New York: Alfred A. Knopf, Inc., 1949.

Index